THE HIGH PEAKS
OF
ENGLAND & WALES

A Hillwalkers' Guide

HILLSIDE GUIDES - ACROSS THE NORTH AND BEYOND

Mountain Walking
- **THE HIGH PEAKS OF ENGLAND & WALES**

Long Distance Walks
- **TRANS-PENNINE WAY**
- **DALES WAY**
- **WESTMORLAND WAY**
- **CUMBERLAND WAY**
- **PENDLE WAY**
- **NORTH BOWLAND TRAVERSE**
- **COAST TO COAST WALK**
- **CLEVELAND WAY**
- **FURNESS WAY**
- **LADY ANNE'S WAY**
- **NIDDERDALE WAY**

Hillwalking - Lake District
- **LAKELAND FELLS, SOUTH**
- **LAKELAND FELLS, NORTH**
- **LAKELAND FELLS, EAST**
- **LAKELAND FELLS, WEST**

Circular Walks - Peak District
- **NORTHERN PEAK**
- **CENTRAL PEAK**
- **WESTERN PEAK**
- **EASTERN PEAK**
- **SOUTHERN PEAK**

Circular Walks - Yorkshire Dales
- **HOWGILL FELLS**
- **MALHAMDALE**
- **NIDDERDALE**
- **SWALEDALE**
- **FREEDOM OF THE DALES** (Large format colour hardback)
- **THREE PEAKS**
- **WHARFEDALE**
- **WENSLEYDALE**

Circular Walks - North York Moors
- **WESTERN MOORS**
- **NORTHERN MOORS**
- **SOUTHERN MOORS**

Circular Walks - South Pennines
- **BRONTE COUNTRY**
- **CALDERDALE**
- **ILKLEY MOOR**
- **SOUTHERN PENNINES**

Circular Walks - Lancashire
- **BOWLAND**
- **WEST PENNINE MOORS**
- **PENDLE & THE RIBBLE**

Circular Walks - North Pennines
- **TEESDALE**
- **EDEN VALLEY**

Yorkshire Pub Walks
- **HARROGATE & THE WHARFE VALLEY**
- **HAWORTH & THE AIRE VALLEY**

- **YORK WALKS** *City Theme Walks*

Send for a detailed catalogue and pricelist

Also by Paul Hannon
- **80 DALES WALKS** (Cordee)
- **25 WALKS - YORKSHIRE DALES** (Stationery Office)

THE HIGH PEAKS OF ENGLAND & WALES

A Hillwalkers' Guide
to the
2500ft mountains

Paul Hannon

HILLSIDE

HILLSIDE PUBLICATIONS
12 Broadlands
Shann Park
Keighley
West Yorkshire
BD20 6HX

First published 1999

© Paul Hannon 1999

ISBN 1 870141 67 9

British Library Cataloguing in Publication Data
A catalogue record for this book is available from the British Library

Front cover: Snowdon from Crib Goch
Back cover: Pillar from Wasdale
Page 1: Bristly Ridge (Glyder Fach) and Tryfan
from Llyn y Caseg-fraith
Page 3: Skiddaw from the summit of Blencathra

The author has walked and researched all of the routes for the purposes of this guide, but no responsibility can be accepted for unforeseen circumstances encountered while following them. While most of the routes mentioned are in regular use by walkers, and many are on public paths, inclusion of a route does not imply that a right of way exists.

Dedicated to
Jagger and his brilliant Bantams, for another 'high peak' of 1999

Printed by Dai Nippon Printing Company (Hong Kong) Ltd

∧ Scafell Pike   THE HIGH SUMMITS   Snowdon∨

CONTENTS

INTRODUCTION

While an increasing number of hillwalkers aspire to reach the summits of the Scottish 'Munros' (mountains over 3000ft/914m), few have similar designs on the 220 'Corbetts' (mountains over 2500ft/762m) north of the border. Much of this is down to relative inaccessibility, and herein lies the attraction of their conveniently placed English and Welsh counterparts. There are 40 mountain peaks in England and Wales that break the 2500ft barrier and also require the minimum 500ft of re-ascent that earns the equivalent of Corbett status. By coincidence both countries boast exactly the same number, 20 each, thus ensuring a balanced coverage.

Inevitably, most of England's candidates are to be found in the Lake District, with token representation from the Pennines and the Cheviots. Indeed no hill in the southern half of the Pennines finds it way in, for Whernside, highest peak in the Yorkshire Dales, reaches only 2415ft/736m. Similarly, the greatest concentration of high peaks in Wales is in Snowdonia, though some hills escape its bounds, and of course the summits of the Brecon Beacons are very much a separate entity. Only three of the peaks (Cross Fell, Mickle Fell and Cadair Berwyn) are to be found outside of the four National Parks of Snowdonia, Lake District, Brecon Beacons and Northumberland.

A small number of English and Welsh peaks also manage to attain the 3000ft mark, and for completeness these are included within the scope of this book, regardless of whether they satisfy the 500ft of re-ascent criterion. Hence the bonus peaks of Scafell and the northern Carneddau have earned their own chapters, these being the only 3000ft peaks not otherwise covered. In view of the dearth of such heights in England and Wales, it is justifiable to accord them due recognition.

Approaching Helvellyn from Great Dodd

Each chapter is devoted to a particular mountain or pair of neighbouring peaks. A description of the principal features includes a summary of the various ascent routes. The second part of each chapter is then given over to a recommended walk taking in the summits. The majority of the walks also include neighbouring hills that not only add to the walk's interest, but provide a more logical route and ultimately a more rewarding day on the hills. This book is emphatically not a list-ticker's 'bible', and while a complete table of the 2500ft mountains is included overleaf, a glance at the book's index will reveal the wealth of other peaks encountered on the main walks.

While completion of the 32 walks will ensure that all the English and Welsh Corbetts and 3000-footers have been climbed, the principal aim of this book is to provide, both in words and in pictures, inspiration for great days on these highest hills.

All of the selected walks should be within the capabilities of experienced hillwalkers in summer, though four (Blencathra, Helvellyn, Snowdon and Tryfan/Glyder Fawr) do feature sections of scrambling. When wet and windy these might prove unnerving for some, but alternative routes are mentioned. Even walkers new to the hills are likely to have some experience of gentler walking, and be already aware of the need for items such as comfortable boots and rucksack, adequate clothing, waterproofs, food and drink. Temperatures on the hills are often appreciably lower than in the valleys even in summer, and a combination of exhaustion and increasing cold can bring on exposure at any time of year: hence the need for additional spare clothing and food, survival bag and a whistle. Map and compass should of course always be carried, for even familiar ground can become confusing in poor visibility.

In winter, any one of these walks can and often will prove an entirely different proposition, and not just on the more obvious scrambles. The winter hillwalker must be prepared not only for the worst conditions, but also know when to turn back. Snow or ice on the hills means ice axe and crampons should be carried and ready for use, and a torch is similarly essential. The greatest cause of mountain accidents is a simple slip on snowy or icy ground - ground that is not always that steep.

The less experienced should remember that items such as compass and ice axe are of little use if their owner doesn't know how to use them. Comprehensive books are available on the subjects of mountain equipment, safety, technique and weather, and those in doubt will find a wealth of information to help prepare them for the more demanding hills.

Inclusion of a route does not imply a right of way exists, though virtually every hill enjoys some form of accepted access: anomalies such as Mickle Fell are explained where necessary. Whether on public paths or not, it behoves every walker to tread as lightly as possible. The popularity of the hills means many paths

Y Garn and Foel-goch reflected in Llyn Ogwen

have been eroded to the point where repair work has become essential, and many hills now carry evidence of more substantial remedies. Outside of winter try to wear as light a pair of boots as possible, feet will feel the benefit as much as the vegetation does. Avoid creating direct scars when sensitive zigzags are in place, whether on an original path or a rebuilt one. Finally, don't encourage the proliferation of unnecessary cairns, a problem prevalent in the Lake District for several decades: while some have historic or important navigational value, the vast majority are an eyesore.

With few exceptions these hills are every bit as impressive as the acclaimed mountains of Scotland: within these pages is a remarkable array of variety and interest, and certainly the high peaks of England and Wales can prove just as demanding and rewarding as their cousins north of the border.

THE HIGH PEAKS OF ENGLAND AND WALES

All summits above 2500ft with a minimum re-ascent of 500ft

		feet	metres				feet	metres	
1	Snowdon (Yr Wyddfa)	3560	1085	....	21	Grasmoor	2795	852	....
2	Carnedd Llewelyn	3491	1064	....	22	Saint Sunday Crag	2760	841	....
3	Glyder Fawr	3278	999	....	23	Cadair Berwyn	2723	830	....
4	Scafell Pike	3209	978	....	24	High Street	2718	828	....
5	Helvellyn	3116	950	....	25	The Cheviot	2674	815	....
6	Y Garn	3107	947	....	26	Waun Fach	2661	811	....
7	Skiddaw	3054	931	....	27	High Stile	2648	807	....
8	Elidir Fawr	3031	924	....	28	Coniston Old Man	2635	803	....
9	Tryfan	3002	915	....	29	Kirk Fell	2631	802	....
10	Aran Fawddwy	2969	905	....	30	Fan Brycheiniog	2631	802	....
11	Great Gable	2949	899	....	31	Pen Llithrig y Wrach	2621	799	....
12	Y Lliwedd	2946	898	....	32	Grisedale Pike	2595	791	....
13	Cross Fell	2930	893	....	33	Mickle Fell	2585	788	....
14	Cadair Idris	2930	893	....	34	Moel Hebog	2569	783	....
15	Pillar	2927	892	....	35	Glasgwm	2559	780	....
16	Pen y Fan	2907	886	....	36	Red Screes	2547	776	....
17	Fairfield	2863	873	....	37	Moelwyn Mawr	2526	770	....
18	Moel Siabod	2861	872	....	38	Waun Rydd	2523	769	....
19	Blencathra	2847	868	....	39	Caudale Moor	2502	763	....
20	Arenig Fawr	2802	854	....	40	High Raise	2500	762	....

SOME USEFUL ADDRESSES

Ramblers' Association
1/5 Wandsworth Road, London SW8 2XX (0171-339 8500)

Youth Hostels Association
Trevelyan House, 8 St. Stephen's Hill, St. Albans AL1 2DY
(01727-55215)

Lake District National Park
Brockhole, Windermere LA23 1LJ (015394-46601)

Northumberland National Park
Eastburn, South Park, Hexham NE46 1BS (01434-605555)

Snowdonia National Park
Penrhyndeudraeth, Gwynedd LL48 6LF (01766-770274)

Brecon Beacons National Park
7 Glamorgan Street, Brecon LD3 7DP (01874-624437)

Rail services - National Enquiry Line (0345-484950)

Mountain Rescue - Dial 999 and request 'Police'

National Park/Tourist Information
England
Railway Station **Alston** (01434-381696)
Market Cross **Ambleside** (015394-32582)
Moot Hall, Boroughgate**Appleby-in-Westmorland**(017683-51177)
Woodleigh, Flatts Road **Barnard Castle** (01833-690909)
Car Park **Coniston** (015394-41533)
Car Park **Glenridding** (017684-82414)

Redbank Road **Grasmere** (015394-35245)
Moot Hall **Keswick** (017687-72645)
Market Street **Kirkby Stephen** (017683-71199)
Penrith Museum, Middlegate **Penrith** (01768-867466)
The Square **Pooley Bridge** (017864-86530)
Victoria Street **Windermere** (015394-46499)
Bus Station Car Park, High Street **Wooler** (01668-281602)
Wales
Monmouth Road **Abergavenny** (01873-857588/853254)
Penllyn, Pensarn Road **Bala** (01678-521021)
Town Hall, Deiniol Road **Bangor** (01248-352786)
Old Library, Station Road **Barmouth** (01341-280787)
Royal Oak Stables **Betws-y-Coed** (01690-710426)
Isallt, High Street **Blaenau Ffestiniog** (01766-830360)
Cattle Market Car Park **Brecon** (01874-622485/623156)
Oriel Pendeitsh, Castle Street **Caernarfon** (01286-672232)
CADW Visitor Centre, Castle Entrance **Conwy** (01492-592248)
Craft Centre **Corris** (01654-761244)
Beaufort Chambers, Beaufort Street **Crickhowell** (01873-812105)
Ty Meirion, Eldon Square **Dolgellau** (01341-422888)
Craig-y-nos Country Park **Glyntawe** (01639-730395)
Oxford Road **Hay-on-Wye** (01497-820144)
Mountain Centre **Libanus** near Brecon (01874-623366)
41A High Street **Llanberis** (01286-870765)
Car Park, Crescent Road **Llandeilo** (01558-824226)
Kings Road **Llandovery** (01550-720693)
Town Hall, Castle Street **Llangollen** (01978-860828)
Canolfan Owain Glyndwr **Machynlleth** (01654-702401)
14a Glebeland Street **Merthyr Tydfil** (01685-379884)
High Street **Porthmadog** (01766-512981)
High Street **Tywyn** (01654-710070)

ENGLAND

Of the twenty Corbetts of England all but three are to be found within the Lake District, but this intimacy does not affect their ability to offer the walker a richly varied tapestry of scenery. The rugged, volcanic heart of the district sees the highest ground in England, Scafell Pike, surrounded by similarly rough peaks such as Great Gable, the Langdale Pikes, the Coniston Fells and Bowfell. Lakeland's finest valleys radiate from this central hub, with Wasdale, Borrowdale, Eskdale and Langdale taking precedence. Pillar and High Stile are summits of magnificent ridges that break up these valleys.

Beyond the delectable Buttermere Valley, the cleaner-cut outlines of predominantly slaty mountains such as the Grasmoor group and then Skiddaw hold sway: the latter boasts the unique mountain of Blencathra among its entourage. To the east of the central divide of Dunmail Raise, long high ridges link neighbouring tops with ease, and include mighty Helvellyn as well as the ever popular Fairfield and High Street.

East of High Street, grassier rolling hills lead towards the Pennines, but the highest ground of the Pennines is far removed, for the highest point of Cross Fell stands beyond the deep divide of the lush Vale of Eden. The North Pennines form an unbroken chain running north to the Tyne Gap, with little in the way of independent summits. Southwards, the Stainmore Gap leads to the more shapely and individual peaks of the Yorkshire Dales, even though none are sufficiently elevated to feature in these pages.

The northernmost high ground in England is found in the Cheviot Hills of Northumberland, rounded tops that overlook the Scottish border. Indeed they share many similarities with the endless sweep of Border Hills that are invariably ignored by hillwalkers heading north to the Highlands.

Lakeland's major centres are Keswick and Ambleside, with Coniston, Patterdale, Buttermere and Wasdale also well placed. Appleby and Kirkby Stephen are convenient for the western edge of the North Pennines, with Middleton in Teesdale a good central base. The small town of Wooler is the best base for the Cheviots.

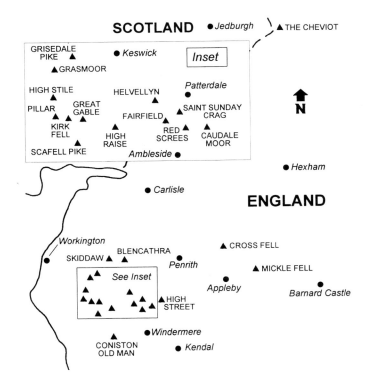

The Cheviot from Housey Crags
Opposite: Scafell Pike across Great Moss, upper Eskdale

BLENCATHRA   2848ft/868m

No mountain in Lakeland puts its goods in the window to better effect than Blencathra, whose magnificent south front presents an arresting profile. Three slim spurs emanate from the summit skyline, each broadening considerably before embracing the valley floor. This handsome trio of Gategill Fell, Hall's Fell and Doddick Fell shelter two rugged, steep-sided gills, while the broad shoulders of Blease Fell and Scales Fell sweep round to enclose the package, each ushering another impressive gill in with it. To the north-west the fell adopts a total change of character, with featureless grassy slopes rolling down to Roughten Gill, and viewers of Blencathra from the fells of Skiddaw Forest may as well be looking at another mountain; certainly many of its devotees would fail to recognise it.

Blencathra is robbed of all round symmetry by a section of the mountain not on obvious display, a little corner that claims the fell's only tarn and its most famous ridge. Scales Tarn lurks in a shaded hollow beneath the well named Sharp Edge, considered by many to be superior to its great rival on Helvellyn. Above it is the neat peak crowning the forbidding Foule Crag, prominent in views from the east and in conjunction with Hallsfell Top, responsible for the mountain's alternative and undeniably descriptive title of Saddleback. The saddle itself is adorned by a memorial cross laid out in dazzling quartz stones.

With such a wealth of ascent routes there is no excuse for treading the same ground twice, though inevitably certain routes stand out above others. Sharp Edge and Hall's Fell are the two favourites, and each offers something different. The appeal of Sharp Edge is only felt on gaining the shore of Scales Tarn, from where the start of the traverse is only minutes away. While not matching Striding Edge in extent, this razor edge demands more handling of rock, and induces a sense of exposure not normally experienced on Helvellyn's equivalent. Wintry, particularly icy, conditions will render the ridge out of bounds to 99% of its summer traffic. Its two distinct sections comprise the spiky turrets of the edge proper, and a steep clamber up a reclined slab.

For sustained interest, the ascent of the Hall's Fell ridge takes the honours. Initially steep but well graded, the ridge proper begins halfway up, narrowing into a transport of delights. Easy angled rock towers offer hands-on interest, and while an alternative lower level path has been worn, it would be almost criminal to use it. Opportunities to ascend a rocky spine such as this are few and far between, and here, more than ever, it's not just a matter of getting there, but also how you get there. The icing on the cake awaits at the top, for the ridge remains robust to the very end, abruptly and unexpectedly terminating at a sprawling cairn that reveals itself as the true summit of the mountain.

Of its companion frontal ridges, Doddick Fell is to be next preferred, being a delightful scaled down version of Hall's Fell, with the advantage of getting onto the ridge early in the climb. Not so Gategill Fell, which demands a more sustained pull to the beckoning outcrop of Knott Halloo. Other commonly used ascent routes take paths up the outer slopes of Blease and Scales Fells, each enlivened in their upper sections by a promenade above spurs and deep gills. High level approaches can be made from Mungrisdale to the north-east, ideally over the summits of neighbouring fells Bowscale Fell and/or Bannerdale Crags.

Disappointment that a classic climb has ended is tempered by the satisfaction of the panorama revealed, although nothing is more impressive than the dramatic downward scene comprising Hall's Fell and the depths of Doddick Gill. Additional attractions include the extensive North Pennines skyline beyond the Eden Valley, and the guarantee of a different descent route, invariably to Threlkeld or Scales from where most ascents spring.

ROUTE 1: BLENCATHRA

Summits:
Blencathra   2848ft/868m

Start: *Scales (NY 342268). A roadside lay-by on the A66 west of the hamlet, just past Toll Bar Cottage at Scales Green. Limited parking in Scales itself, near the White Horse Inn. Served by Penrith-Keswick buses and also seasonal Keswick-Patterdale and Keswick-Mungrisdale services.*

Distance: *4 miles/6½km*

Ascent: *2182ft/665m*

Maps:
OS 1:50,000 - Landranger 90
1:25,000 - Outdoor Leisure 5

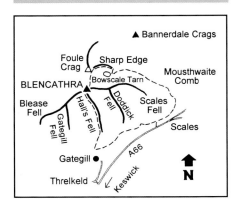

On Blencathra's Hall's Fell ridge, looking east to Doddick Fell and Scales Fell

The base of the fell is gained at Toll Bar Cottage. From a kissing-gate the main path slants up through bracken, leaving the intake wall behind to rise above Mousthwaite Comb. The path then contours around the base of Scales Fell, above some rougher ground to a point just above the Mousthwaite Col. On rounding a corner the next stage of the path can be seen contouring ahead, and at the same time one of the most spectacular sights in Lakeland greets the eye.

This is Foule Crag, its flat top breaking into a sheer drop to the spiky ridge of Sharp Edge. After a good stride the path climbs by the outflow of Scales Tarn to the water's edge, discovering a sombre hollow of great atmosphere. If conditions dictate that Sharp Edge be omitted, then a clear path re-crosses the outflow to slant up the south side of the comb.

From the tarn the path quickly climbs onto the commencement of Sharp Edge, with no problems of route-finding on this infallible and exhilarating guide. Those of a nervous disposition will take advantage, for the most part, of a path to the north below the edge proper, during which time little height is gained. When the spiky turrets cease, all must face a fascinating scramble up a benevolently tilted slab. Above this the drama ends abruptly near the peak crowning Foule Crag, a minor top set back from the edge and rarely visited. A much trodden path heads south across the eastern edge of the saddle to Blencathra's summit cairn, with the main ridge of the mountain stretching away to the west.

The summit perches neatly above the hill's southern face, with the Hall's Fell ridge striking emphatically down from the very cairn. At once this exciting descent route is in the thick of the action, with near-vertical views down into Gate Gill and Doddick Gill. The narrow ridge offers a succession of rocky aretes, with the option of an alternative lower path. Minor scrambles enliven the decline over this rocky spine until the fun promptly ends on a knoll. The steep descent remains enjoyable as it swings south-west towards Threlkeld, ultimately descending to the intake wall.

Without continuing down to Gate Gill (unless bound for Threlkeld village), a good path doubles back east along the base of the fell, to cross the emerging ravine of Doddick Gill. The path resumes to a similar scene at Scaley Beck, where a mini-scramble presents a sting in the tail. Beyond this obstacle the path leads back to the gate where the fell was first gained.

Ascending Sharp Edge

14

SKIDDAW 3054ft/931m

Skiddaw is Lakeland's friendly giant, an affable old buffer who presents a reassuring backdrop to the Keswick scene. Though not a mountain to inspire superlatives, its memorable southerly outline is instantly recognisable in a thousand felltop views, and one that budding fellwalkers learn early in their apprenticeship. To walkers and tourists alike, this is probably the most familiar mountain scene after that of the Langdale Pikes.

Any English mountain that tops 3000ft must have plenty going for it, and Skiddaw has much to offer in a variety of ascent routes and a plethora of subsidiary tops. It occupies a vast tract of country bounded on one side by Bassenthwaite Lake, the Vale of Keswick, and the attendant bustle of Lakeland, while its other side offers a complete contrast in the form of the infrequently explored upland hollow of Skiddaw Forest. The underlying rock is Skiddaw slate, which reputedly makes Skiddaw the oldest mountain in the district. It is easily distinguished in its forays to the surface, though the only notable outcrops are on Dead Crags, north of the summit.

Skiddaw's satellites consist of the linking tops of Carl Side, Long Side and Ullock Pike; trusty sidekick Little Man; and Bakestall, which is accorded some importance due to the presence of Dead Crags. Even the summit of Skiddaw has several little tops along its elevated half-mile crest, though nowhere do the intervening dips exceed a few feet. The highest point is served by an Ordnance Survey column adrift in a sea of erosion, while a view indicator, cairns and numerous shelters litter the slaty surfaced top.

Of the routes of ascent, one stands out as the popular path, and another as the connoisseur's way. The pony track up Spooney Green Lane, around Latrigg and up Jenkin Hill high above Keswick is the time-honoured route, a Victorian favourite and an exceed-ingly easy walk on a path as wide as a dual carriageway, yet not as tortuous as many lesser used paths in the district. The classic route, meanwhile, sets off from the opposite direction, and climbs the multi-topped ridge of Longside Edge.

In between these two are several alternatives, including steeper approaches up the front from Millbeck and Applethwaite, again with the option of including subsidiary tops; or from the rear by way of the Dash Valley and Bakestall. These northern flanks also hide little used approaches through the delightful side valleys of Barkbethdale and Southerndale, foreign names to the majority of Skiddaw's visitors. Yet another untracked option is to climb the featureless flank above Skiddaw House, a former shepherd's bothy now operating as an exceedingly remote youth hostel.

ROUTE 2: SKIDDAW

Summits:
Long Side   2408ft/734m
Carl Side   2447ft/746m
Skiddaw   3054ft/931m

Start: High Side (NY 236309). A prominent parking area along the minor road to Orthwaite, a quarter-mile off the A591. The main road is served by Keswick-Carlisle buses.

Distance: 9 miles/14½km   **Ascent:** 2900ft/884m

Maps:
OS 1:50,000 - Landranger 89 or 90. 1:25,000 - Outdoor Leisure 4

Just yards beyond the lay-by, towards Barkbeth, a grassy bridlepath begins a zigzag climb through lush pastures. From the outset this old drove road is overlooked by the dark heights of Skiddaw and the enticing crest of Ullock Pike, while Bassenthwaite Lake occupies a deep trench below. The open fell is soon gained above Southerndale Beck, a grand moment. The track into this valley haven is at once vacated to gain a foothold on the welcoming ridge, a veritable stairway to heaven. First feature of note is Watches, a curious arrangement of boulders on a saddle. Beyond, a thin path quickly becomes clearer as the slopes gain both height and form amid the heather and bilberry of the knobbly ridge known as The Edge. Sweeping views over glistening Bassenthwaite Lake contrast with the massive grey bulk of Skiddaw as steps are drawn to the beckoning peak of Ullock Pike.

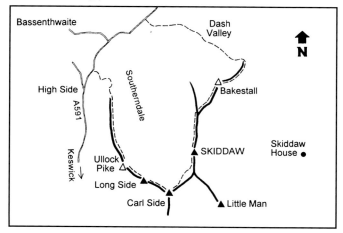

Set a few yards back, the cairn of this minor top occupies a windswept perch above the eastern flank rolling majestically down to Southerndale, backed by the powerful mass of Skiddaw. The other side reveals Bassenthwaite Lake in unparalleled splendour, with the Coledale Fells beyond, marshalled by the striking Grisedale Pike. A few short minutes of first-class fellwalking lead along the

ridge to the greater top of Long Side, whose cairn perches on a luxuriant couch above an extremely steep drop into Southerndale. Away from the permanent gaze of Skiddaw there is a wonderful panorama of every type of country, from the Solway Firth and the many miles of coastline inland to Bassenthwaite Lake and a host of mountain tops ranged across the centre of the district.

Resuming, the path skirts the Southerndale rim to the tiny pool of Carlside Tarn. Collectors of summits will first strike out to take in the rounded top of Carl Side. This is the highest but least interesting of the ascent ridge's three tops. Its advantage over Long Side and Ullock Pike is its south-facing front, and the view from the cairn in its sea of grass can be improved by wandering a little further to the south. A better foreground is afforded to the magnificent mountain prospect south and west of Derwentwater. Another ascent path is met at the cairn, which leads back to the merging of paths by the tarn.

The final stage of the ascent takes shape as the path slants obliquely across Skiddaw's scree-draped upper flank. Looking back, the earlier ascent ridge now seems dwarfed. Although this upper

Skiddaw seen across Derwentwater from Catbells

section steepens towards the top, the path makes relatively light work of things to suddenly ease at a shelter on the airy summit ridge. A two-minute saunter north along the broad, high-level ridge leads quickly to the Ordnance Survey column on the summit of Skiddaw, lowest member of Lakeland's exclusive '3000' club.

While one naturally expects to feel uplifted at this altitude, there is a keener awareness of this on Skiddaw's exposed top, due to the mountain's isolation from similarly high ground. This also guarantees an excellent picture of Lakeland's various mountain groups to the south. Other aspects of the panorama vary from the belt of trees sheltering lonely Skiddaw House deep in the bowl of Skiddaw Forest, to an extensive coastline from the Solway Firth out to the Irish Sea, across which the Galloway Hills and the Isle of Man can look very close on clear days.

Resuming north past more shelters, the route over Broad End and Bakestall appears below. A prolonged descent begins by passing above Gibraltar Crag on the left and down to a plateau. This is the only point where the path is unclear, but a couple of cairns point the way to a fence on the right to descend to Bakestall. Beyond an old sheepfold in the minor col, a cairn at the fence corner sends a path 100 yards out to Bakestall's lower cairn for a splendid view over the Dash Valley.

Though Skiddaw offers little in the way of cliffs, at 2000 feet on these northern slopes begins the spectacular plunge of Dead Crags. Returning towards the fence reveals a wall of crag and scree on a scale not anticipated. An easy descent of Birkett Edge then drops onto the rough road serving Skiddaw House. The road winds down beneath Dead Crags, and only on levelling out are the effervescent Dash Falls revealed back to the right. The Dash Farm road leads out through pastures to the Orthwaite road at Peter House. Virtually traffic-free, with leafy hedgerows and increasingly good views over the day's fells, this makes a relaxing conclusion.

Long Side and Ullock Pike from the entrance to Southerndale

GRASMOOR 2795ft/852m
GRISEDALE PIKE 2595ft/791m

Grasmoor is the loftiest mountain in the north-western fells, yet is an outlier of its own massif. Standing aside from the busy pedestrian thoroughfares, it is one of the least visited summits of the group. The link with high ground is the no-man's-land above Coledale Hause which it shares with Eel Crag. On three sides Grasmoor throws down flanks of crag and scree, the finest aspect overlooking Crummock Water to the west where Grasmoor End dominates the pastures of Lanthwaite Green. To north and south Gasgale Gill and Rannerdale Beck respectively delineate the fell's boundaries.

The most practicable ascent route sets forth from Cinderdale Common above Crummock Water to gain the prominent cairn on Lad Hows, from where a ridge takes shape to lead to the summit acres. A surprisingly seldom used route is the direct climb from Coledale Hause, an obvious line that trades the tedium of the worn path to the Eel Crag col for a riveting picture of Gasgale Gill and Gasgale Crags.

In common with many steep-sided mountains, Grasmoor's higher ground is extensive, being a vast plateau ranging a mile from east to west. The summit is located only a few strides from rough slopes aiming for Rannerdale, and is occupied by a shelter of intricate curves. Grasmoor's major outbreak of cliffs occurs high on its northern flank, Dove Crags being well seen from the route from Coledale Hause, or more completely from the Whiteside ridge across Gasgale Gill. As an all-round viewpoint Grasmoor excels, and from its edges many of Lakeland's mountain groupings are well seen. In addition, it boasts a very extensive sweep of

the Solway Firth, backed on a clear day by the Galloway Hills, with the Isle of Man floating in the Irish Sea. Inland are views beyond Lakeland to the Pennine landmarks of Cross Fell, high above the Eden Valley, and Ingleborough, in the Yorkshire Dales.

From every angle Grisedale Pike presents an elegant outline, a classic profile that is nowhere better illustrated than from the eastern shore of Derwentwater. This is the loftiest peak on the splendid ridge separated from the larger group of Grasmoor fells by Coledale Hause. Coledale forms the base of the fell from the valley head down to Braithwaite at its foot, while to the north a labyrinth of smaller valleys are choked by the heavy afforestation of Whinlatter. At the head of Coledale is the ravaged cliff scenery of Force Crag, with waterfalls, a hanging valley and the remains of mining operations.

Grisedale Pike's pyramid draws almost all of its visitors from Braithwaite, by way of Kinn and Sleet How on the tiered east ridge. With a relentless fall from cairn to Coledale the southern face is out of bounds, but the northern aspect merits a second glance. Two lonely ridges struggle free from the forest to merge near the summit, and offer an obvious half-day's circular route far from the crowds.

Two superb ridges also climb from the Vale of Lorton, though both belong to neighbouring peaks attached to Grisedale Pike. Least known is the Swinside ridge, a largely heathery pull to Ladyside Pike preceding the beautiful cone of Hopegill Head; more popular is a wonderful ridge above Lanthwaite Green, traversing Whiteside en route to Hopegill Head.

Grisedale Pike is a fine, exposed mountain top, with a view that is unquestionably one of Lakeland's finest. The juxtaposition of Hobcarton Crag on one side and the Derwentwater scene on the other is a stunning contrast, while to the south-east is a skyline in which a shapely cluster of the great peaks contest elbow room.

ROUTE 3: GRASMOOR & GRISEDALE PIKE

Summits:
Grisedale Pike   2595ft/791m
Hobcarton Crag   2425ft/739m
Grasmoor   2795ft/852m
Wandope   2533ft/772m
Eel Crag   2753ft/839m
Sail   2536ft/773m

Start: *Braithwaite (NY 230236). Careful parking places in the village, and a small car park on the Whinlatter road. Served by Keswick-Cockermouth buses and seasonal Keswick-Buttermere buses.*

Distance: 9½ miles/15km   **Ascent:** 3825ft/1166m

Maps:
OS 1:50,000 - Landranger 89 or 90.   1:25,000 - Outdoor Leisure 4

Braithwaite is departed by the Whinlatter Pass road, as far as a parking area at the base of the fell. A narrow path climbs away, soon merging into a broader one before rising through bracken onto the spacious green ridge of Kinn. The steep pull is relieved by views back over the grey and white houses of Braithwaite to the Vale of Keswick, backed by the mass of the Skiddaw group.

The entire ascent is also in prospect, with an impressive array of peaks hemming in the deep valley of Coledale. First task is the pleasurable one of attaining the top of Grisedale Pike, which shines like a beacon ahead. After a few more hundred feet the heathery crest of Sleet How is gained, and the finest section of this east ridge draws the eager walker up through a slaty stairway which invites modest scrambles for a fitting conclusion to the ascent.

Grasmoor from Gasgale Gill

From this airy, windswept crown a well-blazed path heads south-west along the slaty ridge, though its decline is soon halted when faced by the modest summit of Hobcarton Crag. A short pull gains this intervening top, and within 100 yards of resuming the descent a major fork is reached.

The main route takes the left arm, which sets a direct course for Coledale Hause: it drops steadily past old mineshafts to gain the grassy saddle. For the energetic, the inviting right branch clings to the rim of the Hobcarton Valley, rising with little effort above the dramatic cliffs of Hobcarton Crag to gain the slender summit of Hopegill Head. From this superb location a path returns south-east over the minor top of Sand Hill to descend to the direct route on Coledale Hause.

Just 100 yards across Coledale Hause is a fork, where both arms rise steadily away. The right branch runs on to meet the upper reaches of Gasgale Gill, and absorbing another path, this climbs in the tamed company of the stream towards the no-man's-land between the broad backs of Eel Crag and Grasmoor. This can be abandoned almost at once, however, by crossing the stream to commence a near pathless trek up the defined edge behind, through occasional boulders to gain the rim of the comb below Dove Crags.

By this stage a thin path forms, and the crags are rounded to gain Grasmoor's vast summit plateau. The top is marked by a shapely shelter some distance to the west, nearer the southern face: a slight, cairned line might be found pointing to this edge, where a broad path is joined contouring west towards the summit.

Descending to Sail from Eel Crag, with the Helvellyn range on the skyline

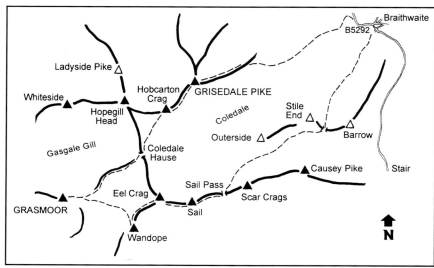

From Grasmoor's top the only lines of descent that appear less than vertical involve heading back eastwards, this time on the much used path along the southern edge, overlooking Crummock Water. This path declines only gently at first, but as more of Eel Crag comes into view a steeper descent is made to the upland depression between the two mountains. Here is a crossroads of paths by a brace of tiny pools, with the obvious route to Eel Crag climbing directly ahead. This short pull up featureless slopes can be greatly improved by taking a thinner path half-right to effortlessly bring the top of Wandope into the day's bag. The summit cairn hovers unassumingly close to an emphatic drop into Addacomb Hole.

Wandope is linked to Eel Crag by a fine walk above Addacomb Hole. A path skirts the rim of this hanging valley, clinging tight on the ascent before rising left to gain Eel Crag's summit. An Ordnance Survey column crowns the highest point of a bare, slaty top on which paths have made little impression. Also known as Crag Hill, this second summit in the Grasmoor group shakes off its 'bridesmaid' tag with its greater geographical superiority over Grasmoor. Eel Crag's pivotal role makes it kingpin of the fells south of Coledale Hause, despite being the only major top in the group without a valley foothold.

Craggy slopes line the north-east and south edges of the plateau, though with care, in mist, they also act as infallible guides to the commencement of the one line of descent in this direction. The way off is indicated by a cairn south-east of the OS column, a good path adhering to the narrow ridge which wastes no time in losing height over short sections of exposed rock. The rounded top of Sail is gained beyond a minor col, though its summit cairn stands to the north of the path and is invariably bypassed. This apologetic pile of stones need not be approached to enhance the excellent mountain panorama from Skiddaw through the heart of the district to the western fells.

From Sail the high-level ridge takes another step nearer the valley by falling to Sail Pass. The broad path down to it is dull after the drop off Eel Crag, but uninterrupted views over Newlands and the Vale of Keswick amply compensate. Sail Pass is a well defined junction of ways, and an inviting option is to cling to high ground as long as possible, remaining on the ridge over Scar Crags and Causey Pike to descend to the Braithwaite-Buttermere road at Stonycroft, a good mile and a half south of Braithwaite.

A more direct and exceptionally easy finish takes the clear path branching north from the pass. This slants beneath the rough flank, with crags and heather above and scree below. The descent eases out after passing an old cobalt mine to reach the saddle of High Moss as a super path. The broadening path is the former mine road that served the workings, and if followed throughout, will lead unfailingly down Stonycroft Gill to the road above Stair. Another option is to complete the true Coledale Horseshoe by taking in the lower tops of Outerside, Stile End and Barrow.

The main route remains on the mine road a little further, until beyond the pyramid of Outerside up to the left. As the track begins a uniform descent, a path branches left, and keeps rigidly to the same contour, passing above a sheepfold. The flank of Stile End is rounded for the last few yards to another path junction in the heathery defile of Barrow Door. Heading straight through the pass, a relaxed stroll down a green swathe through bracken can be enjoyed. The access road to the abandoned farm of High Coledale is utilised for the final half-mile to emerge by the Coledale Inn.

If at Barrow Door the colourful little fell of Barrow tempts a final top to be added, then a well worn path heads straight up the broad ridge to its summit cairn. The north ridge pointing to Braithwaite is the royal road down, first through heather and then bracken, every step being absolute joy. Ultimately leaving the fell above Braithwaite Lodge, the farm road leads down to the edge of the village.

HIGH STILE 2648ft/807m

Dividing the western valleys of Buttermere and Ennerdale is a great mountain wall dominated by High Stile, central and loftiest peak on this archetypal Lakeland ridge. This is a classic mountain study: steep, untrodden slopes falling south to the Ennerdale plantations, and arms branching east and west to the two subsidiary tops of High Crag and Red Pike. To the north a rim of crags guard the felltop, overlooking two combs, each shared with one of its companions. In between, a formidable buttress projects high above Buttermere, this jewel of a lake which laps the base of the mountain.

The felltop is surprisingly broad, but remains rough and stony. A perambulation of the northern edge sees a view already one of Lakeland's finest (with the Gable and Pillar groups ranged across Ennerdale) exalted to classic status when the sensational plunges into the combs add depth to pictures of Buttermere and Fleetwith Pike, and Crummock Water and Grasmoor respectively. Though never approaching knife-edge proportions, the ridge linking with High Stile's staunch supporters is a joy to tread if the walker keeps to the escarpments. Each comb shelters beneath some outstanding cliffs, with Chapel Crags above Bleaberry Comb and Eagle Crag above Burtness Comb, a climbers' favourite.

The most regular routes onto High Stile entail tackling one of its supporting shoulders first, Red Pike from the west, High Crag from the east. The ascent over High Crag begins from Scarth Gap Pass, reached from Buttermere, Gatesgarth, or Black Sail Hut at the head of Ennerdale. The minor top of Seat is breasted to face up to one of Lakeland's more daunting clambers up the purgatorial Gamlin End onto High Crag, though remarkable restoration work has benefitted walkers as much as the beleaguered vegetation.

The steep ascent from Buttermere by way of Red Pike is a favourite in its own right. Climbing by Sour Milk Gill to Bleaberry Comb, the waters of Bleaberry Tarn offer respite before the dusty haul up to the summit. That this path's erosion was noted by Wainwright in the 1960s is proof enough of its popularity. Red Pike can also be pleasurably gained by way of heathery Lingcomb Edge, on a far more rewarding walk that first incorporates Scale Force.

For a direct approach to High Stile, then Burtness Comb is the key to a hugely satisfying ascent. From the foot of Buttermere a path escapes the trees to rise to the lip of the comb, after which this pleasurable adventure takes to the impending north-east ridge. The views are excellent throughout, and the climb less demanding than might be anticipated. From Gillerthwaite youth hostel in Ennerdale a solitary break in the forestry permits an old sheep droving way to gain the fellside between Red Pike and Starling Dodd, and the direct if featureless continuation onto Red Pike has the one distinction of saving the glorious Buttermere views until the very last moment.

Left: A walker descending from Lingcomb Edge on Red Pike, looking across Crummock Water to the Grasmoor group

ROUTE 4: HIGH STILE

Summits:
High Stile   2648ft/807m
Red Pike   2477ft/755m

Start: Buttermere (NY 175169). Two village centre car parks. Summer bus service from Keswick (via Whinlatter and Borrowdale).

Distance: 6½ miles/10½km   **Ascent:** 2477ft/755m

Maps:
OS 1:50,000 - Landranger 89. 1:25,000 - Outdoor Leisure 4

A fenced track runs left of the Fish Hotel and along to the foot of Buttermere, where up ahead, Sourmilk Gill cascades through the trees and High Stile waits high on the skyline. Crossing the lake's outflow and Sourmilk Gill, a broad path runs along the shore. After just 100 yards a branch slants up to the right, gaining easy height in Burtness Wood. About 100 yards beyond a parallel wall and beck, a thin green trod heads off to the right, soon leaving the wood at a stile. At once the views open out over Buttermere to the Dale Head group, and more impressively Fleetwith Pike.

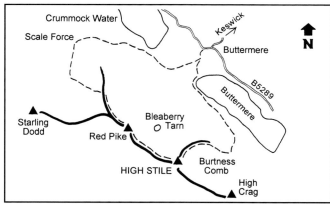

Not very well worn, this super path runs a near level course left. As a wall comes in for company, it rises as a green way through bracken to approach Burtness Comb. Up above, High Crag thrusts a massive buttress forward, soon joined by the crags overlooking the amphitheatre of Burtness Comb. On parting company with the wall, the main path swings right rather than entering the comb, setting its sights on High Stile's currently ill-defined north-east ridge.

High Stile from Fleetwith Pike, showing the north-east ridge

The path swings off right again, on a grand course at an undemanding gradient towards the Buttermere side of the ridge. Climbing through tussocky heather, a rib of modest outcrops neatly delineate the edge of the curving ridge as Buttermere's lake is joined by Crummock Water, with the Grasmoor fells grouped behind the village. When Red Pike is revealed across Bleaberry Comb, it is quickly joined by Bleaberry Tarn cradled on the floor of this hanging valley. The uppermost section offers a final boss of rock, the gateway to an extensive top. By now Great Gable, the Scafells and Pillar are arrayed over the ridge from High Crag. The path falters before moving onto the centrally placed summit cairn.

A line of cairns point the way to merge with old fenceposts bound for the western edge of High Stile's top, crowned by a cairn on a rocky edge. This is a first-class vantage point, with Bleaberry Tarn in its comb far below, and Red Pike pushing elegantly skyward. This splendid top is the next objective, with a good path linking the two mountains. A short, stony descent leads down to an impressive stance at the head of Chapel Crags Gully. A short grassy stroll precedes the gentlest of rises, swinging right up onto Red Pike's small top.

Of many fine fells ranged above Buttermere, this shapely peak claims the greatest affinity. Its top juts out with prominence from the ridge, but the severity of its face is such that the summit is out of sight from the village centre. This airy perch is exposed and barren, with a sprawl of stones struggling to succeed as either cairn or shelter. Classic features of the panorama are the aerial view of Bleaberry Tarn backed by High Stile, and the more complete picture of Crummock Water and the scree-draped Grasmoor fells. The inclusion of Buttermere, Loweswater, Ennerdale Water and Derwentwater makes this one of the finest 'lakes' viewpoints.

Descent begins with a zigzag down easy screes to the start of Lingcomb Edge. A branch left on the watershed towards the dome of Starling Dodd is ignored in favour of the well defined

Red Pike rises above Bleaberry Tarn, seen from High Stile

edge path. On reaching the heather zone, a broad path branches off the edge, doubling back before descending to Scale Beck. Turning downstream it takes in an attractive, confined section until a stony path merges from above. Below this the stream enters a wooded ravine in readiness for its moment of glory at Scale Force. Paths lead down either side of the beck, the more popular right branch stays closer to it to reach the bridge at the foot of the falls. The shy waterfall makes an impressive sight if venturing the few yards nearer to gain a better glimpse into its secretive ravine.

Beyond Scale Force the path heads off through a gateway, keeping well above marshy terrain near the head of Crummock Water. Eventually it drops down nearer the lake to recommence at a lower level. Without ever reaching the shore the path runs beneath the woods above the alluvial plain between Crummock Water and Buttermere, and accompanies the linking Buttermere Dubs towards the latter. Midway along it is spanned by the stone arched Scale Bridge, and by crossing it the walk ends in the way it began, along a fenced lane back into the village.

PILLAR 2926ft/892m
KIRK FELL 2631ft/802m

One of the country's most respected mountains is also one of its least accessible, for attempts on Pillar are usually made from the vehicular cul-de-sac of Wasdale Head. While Pillar appears impressive at the head of Mosedale, it reserves its true nature for the much less frequented Ennerdale. Here the mountain assumes magnificent proportions, and, along with Great Gable at the very dalehead, completely dominates the valley. Such is its position that the scene is best appreciated from the valley head early in the day, before shadows are cast on the great line of crags, coves and rough fellside.

The feature that named the mountain occupies a prime site on this north face. With cliff faces to east and west, Pillar Rock is one of the grandest objects in the district. Pillar is the highest of Lakeland's least visited mountain group, which also includes such fine specimens as Steeple, Red Pike and Yewbarrow. The latter two are grouped around the short valley of Mosedale, while the likes of Haycock, Seatallan and Iron Crag spread further afield.

The Mosedale skyline is a classic horseshoe walk which involves some mild scrambling on the crossing of Yewbarrow, then easy ascents over Red Pike, Scoat Fell and Black Crag; from Pillar the true horseshoe would continue across Black Sail Pass onto Kirk Fell before returning to Wasdale. Relative difficulty of access to Ennerdale sees few approaches from its forest, but one of the very finest is by the ridge of Steeple, leading to Pillar by way of Scoat Fell and Black Crag.

Black Sail Pass is the springboard for most approaches, though only the occupants of Black Sail Hut youth hostel are in a position to take advantage from the head of lonely Ennerdale. The pass is traditionally gained via a steep climb by Gatherstone Beck from Wasdale Head via Mosedale, and from its crest two contrasting routes await. The direct one is a stroll along the bulky east ridge, the other is one of the finest walkers' paths in Lakeland. The High Level Route leaves the broad ridge under Looking Stead to enjoy a remarkable traverse across the coves to its sole original destination, Pillar Rock. Here the ledge of the Shamrock Traverse precedes a mildly scrambly pull directly onto the summit.

First time visitors to Pillar will be surprised at the flatness of the highest ground. This broad summit demands an exploration of its rim, where fine aspects await of Ennerdale Water, Scoat Fell and Steeple, and of course the emphatic plunge of the Ennerdale face; Robinson's Cairn can easily be located many hundreds of feet below, while the Rock cannot be missed.

A route onto the fell that might initially appear bizarre, is in practice logical and undemanding. Though few would connect Honister Pass with Pillar, well trodden paths link the summit of the pass with Black Sail Pass. Honister's advantages over Wasdale are its accessibility and its altitude of almost 1200ft/365m, while the walking by way of the Drum House, Moses' Trod, Beck Head and Kirk Fell's north traverse is relatively effortless. On the return, fit walkers have the tantalising prospect of Kirk Fell, Great Gable, Green Gable and Brandreth to give a memorable mountain day.

Kirk Fell is the patron fell of Wasdale, an uncomplicated bulk dividing the heads of Wasdale and Ennerdale and the more illustrious mountains of Pillar and Great Gable. Ranged across the passes of Black Sail and Beck Head respectively, this pair of peaks syphon off most potential climbers, and with the Scafell group equally accessible from Wasdale Head, Kirk Fell enjoys peace.

The fell is uniformly steep on all flanks, but rather than tapering to a peak to rival Gable, the slopes falter at a crucial stage, resulting in a top so extensive that it forms two different summits. The higher one marks the culmination of the only direct ascent route, a relentless assault from Wasdale Head recommended largely for its views.

Alternative ways on or off connect with the two passes. That from Beck Head is a fairly short pull up the crag-supported Rib End, while the more interesting Black Sail route is a highly enjoyable minor scramble if the lingering fenceposts are religiously traced. A gem of a path traverses the north flank of the mountain from pass to pass, and though of little use in gaining the summit, it offers striking views up to the dark pinnacled cliffs of Kirkfell Crags.

In spite of its girth this is a superb viewpoint, with Wastwater and its Screes and the Scafell grouping well seen. Pride of place goes to Great Gable, whose proximity exaggerates its grotesquely contorted form from this unique angle, as if the top few hundred feet have been twisted like the top of a paper bag.

Pillar Rock from Robinson's Cairn

ROUTE 5: PILLAR & KIRK FELL

Summits:
Kirk Fell   2631ft/802m
Pillar   2926ft/892m

Start: *Wasdale Head (NY 187088). There is a spacious triangular green just before the road runs its final yards to the centre of the hamlet.*

Distance: *7½ miles/12km*   **Ascent:** *3592ft/1095m*

Maps:
OS 1:50,000 - Landranger 89 or 90. 1:25,000 - Outdoor Leisure 4 & 6

From the green a narrow lane leads into the hamlet, and by the far side of the Wasdale Head Inn a path runs upstream with Mosedale Beck past a fine example of a packhorse bridge. Pillar tops the fells beyond, but more imminent is the uncompromising stance of Kirk Fell. At the end the base of the open fell is gained, and the no-nonsense ascent begins. As the Black Sail path bears off left, a less genteel path tackles Kirk Fell's unrelenting contours. While the Wasdale Head scene is outstanding from the outset, the stunning array of peaks surrounding this famous dalehead makes amends for the sweat and toil.

Ultimately a grassy knoll ensures a welcome halt, then the upper section leads into inescapable scree. The path scrabbles ungainly up steep rivers of stones before a grateful escape onto grass. A higher level scree section is far less intimidating, and this leads to a small but inviting arete. Atop this the going eases and the grassy slope is virtually pathless as cairns guide the way onto the extensive top. The summit is straight ahead, a circular shelter occupying the highest point with a cairn on lower ground 25 yards to its north.

Leaving north-west over easy ground, the remains of old fenceposts accompany a path to the edge of Kirkfell Crags. A more cautious descent of this rough, steep section leads down to the grassy saddle of the Black Sail Pass, with Pillar beyond. The crest of the pass is marked by a junction of paths, an incongruous iron gate, and, to the Wasdale side, a large cairn.

Accompanied by fenceposts a steadily rising path heads west along the ridge. This largely avoids the dramatic northern edge until reaching a well defined saddle overlooking it, where the fenceposts return after they drop back down from the minor top Looking Stead. Here a steeper climb begins, breaking its pull on a small knoll where a prominent cairn indicates the start of the High Level Route going off to the right. The easiest option remains on the ridge, and sets about the immediately steeper section in front.

The High Level Route commences rather unconvincingly by dropping down, and certainly it seems to steer an improbable course across this craggy face, but after just a few downhill yards it settles down to a generally undulating route. A variety of terrain is encountered, from grassy terraces to sensational moments above steep drops into Ennerdale. The going becomes gentler on entering bouldery Hind Cove, at the end of which the guiding beacon of Robinson's Cairn stands proud.

The touching of this edifice is a stirring moment as the mighty Pillar Rock appears across Pillar Cove, projecting itself high above Ennerdale. As the path sets off it dips across the cove, with some fine pinnacles towering above. After a short climb through scree it turns right along the broad, tilted ledge of Shamrock Traverse, before a clamber up the side of a sloping slab. Atop this the path arrives at a splendid viewing station on equal terms with the rockface.

A little terrace leads round to the neck of land where the Rock is attached to the face of the mountain. From here the path turns to enjoy an enjoyable climb to the summit, these last few hundred feet proving to be a first-class finale. When faced with a short scramble up a gully, an easier option goes right and curves up to gain the plateau edge at a shelter, but the scramble makes a more appropriate conclusion. The going suddenly relents and the path eases itself onto Pillar's surprisingly extensive summit area. A multi-angled shelter built in the centre marks the highest point some 60 yards away, alongside an Ordnance Survey column and a cairn.

Departing to the south-east, a path forms within yards, aided by fenceposts. In good weather awesome views peer over the northern edges, not all of which are seen if holding to the path, which keeps generally close to the line of defunct fenceposts during this extended amble down the east ridge to Black Sail Pass. With a good mile of the ridge underfoot the Looking Stead col is regained,

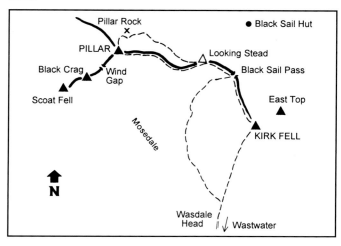

An evening descent of Kirk Fell, looking to the Scafell group

and the fenceposts can be followed up onto the grassy summit dome. The cairned top awaits just one minute from the main path, and makes a perfect viewing platform for Pillar Rock's setting.

On the crest of Black Sail Pass the return path heads south, quickly setting about a rough descent towards Mosedale. A series of zigzags work down to cross Gatherstone Beck, then some easier going slants down to the base of the fell. The path now meanders more leisurely along the edge of Mosedale to Wasdale Head.

GREAT GABLE 2949ft/899m

Regardless of the quality of the competition, Great Gable is a full member of the Premier League. No other Lakeland peak so draws the eye, nor exerts such a mystical influence on the walker in the valley. Its famous Wasdale aspect is so easily identifiable it was adopted for the National Park symbol. On its three other sides the mountain presents a different outline, its top rather more rounded, but never mistaken for anything else. Gable's dominance is best illustrated when viewed from the numerous summits of eastern Lakeland, when the famous dome raises itself high above its contemporaries.

Gable's finest features are its cliffs, and with the exception of the brooding Gable Crag, they occur in remarkable fashion on the steep Wasdale flank. Centrepiece is the Great Napes, protruding from the face of the mountain in a series of cliffs and gullies, at the foot of which is the immortalised Napes Needle. The Needle is one of the easier of countless climbs available on this hallowed patch, where names like Tophet Bastion and Eagle's Nest Ridge add further glamour to an already glamorous sport. The Great Napes is cast into isolation by the scree shoots of Great and Little Hell Gates, with lesser crags continuing on each side.

Nearer Sty Head are the cliffs of Kern Knotts, while perched above the Great Napes are Westmorland Crags, beneath the Westmorland Cairn on the edge of the summit. Climbers' tracks skirting the base of many of these crags have merged to create the South Traverse, a route open to adventurous walkers wishing to inspect Gable's prize features at close hand. It runs from Sty Head towards the col of Beck Head, though most choose to strike off it from the Great Napes for a dramatic clamber to the summit. For the devotee of Lakeland's rough places, it is a must.

Walkers intent on the less demanding target of the summit have a wealth of well trodden routes available. Most of these come together at three famous saddles: Sty Head (from Wasdale or Borrowdale), Beck Head (from Wasdale, Ennerdale, Gatesgarth or Honister), and Windy Gap (from Ennerdale, Gatesgarth, Honister or Borrowdale). Sty Head is one of the best known foot passes in the district, and from here springs the once toilsome slog of the Breast Route, now a skilfully restored path. From Styhead Tarn the hollow of Aaron Slack leads a path up to Windy Gap, from where the final few hundred feet are an arduous clamber over a surface that would do the top of Scafell Pike proud.

From Beck Head, the steep climb up a welcome series of zigzags by Gable Crag probably causes less suffering than any other route. Windy Gap can also be reached from the head of Ennerdale, or over Green Gable from Honister or from Seathwaite via Sourmilk Gill. Easiest start of all is Honister Pass, much of the route taking in a good section of Moses' Trod. This old pony route and smuggler's way links Honister with Wasdale Head, and skirting the flanks of Brandreth and Green Gable it can be left either for Windy Gap or at Beck Head. This old way can also be used to reach Beck Head by ascending Gavel Neese from Wasdale Head.

Great Gable's summit is crowned by a final upthrust of rock, and a plaque records the gift of this and surrounding fells to the nation in memory of members of the Fell & Rock Climbing Club who gave their lives in the Great War: a service is conducted each November. While the complete panorama is quite superb, the Scafell massif will always demand most attention. When the summit is busy, discerning walkers flee south to the sanctuary of the Westmorland Cairn. This precariously balanced edifice is a famous landmark, its virtues as a viewpoint self-evident as it overlooks the deep trough of Wasdale.

Right: Descending Great Gable's western spur to Beck Head, with Pillar overtopping Kirk Fell

ROUTE 6: GREAT GABLE

Summits:
Base Brown   2119ft/646m
Green Gable   2628ft/801m
Great Gable   2949ft/899m

Start: *Seathwaite (NY 235121). The road-end at Seathwaite is a mile off the B5289 at Seatoller. Roadside verge parking on the approach to the farm. Seatoller is served by bus from Keswick.*

Distance: *5½ miles/9km*   **Ascent:** *2855ft/870m*

Maps:
OS 1:50,000 - Landranger 89 or 90. 1:25,000 - Outdoor Leisure 4

The farmyard is left by passing beneath the outbuildings, where an enclosed way runs to a footbridge on the river Derwent. Base Brown towers immediately above, but more impending is the prospect of the climb by Sourmilk Gill. A largely rebuilt stairway displays miraculous restoration work, and this direct assault enjoys a very entertaining climb with a brief hands-on section and good views of the waterslides.

At the top the path runs to a gate in a sturdy wall before rising more gently. The beck is rejoined briefly for a final waterfall, then the going eases to arrive at the rim of the hanging valley of Gillercomb. Directly across is the mighty Raven Crag, known to climbers as Gillercomb Buttress. The main path runs a clear course across the basin before climbing to the valley head, but far more rewarding is the inclusion of Base Brown. This carries the double bonus of breaking up the climbing and escaping the crowds.

The level path is left to strike left up grassy slopes towards the nose-end of the fell, aiming for the base of the skyline crag. As the going steepens a massive boulder is passed to find a level path running beneath the crag. This runs left beneath the perched rock of the Hanging Stone, also enjoying a bird's-eye view of the Seathwaite scene. Within yards the crag abates to permit a simple clamber over easy-angled slabs, then a thin, clear path makes a steady rise onto the summit.

The cairn appears backed by Green Gable, itself overtopped by the upper contours of Great Gable. Base Brown's location among the high fells but in the pocket of one valley leaves it with an unbalanced view, though the good bits are very good. The Scafells are ranged splendidly across the gulf of Sty Head, with Lingmell seamed by the dark ravine of Piers Gill; Black Crag flaunts an impressive profile to the left of Pillar, while the cliff of Gillercomb Buttress excites on Grey Knotts.

Resuming towards the Gables, a thin path runs along to rejoin the main path at a grassy col. A steady rise past a line of cairns leads to the main ridge, where the path from Honister Pass is joined. New revelations to the west include Crummock Water and the Grasmoor fells. In the company of a ludicrous number of cairns it is a short pull onto the top of Green Gable. This stunning moment sees the parent fell appear in all its glory, with the awesome prospect of mighty Gable Crag looming quite intimidatingly.

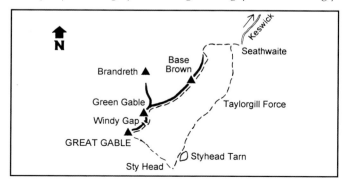

Green Gable, though an underling of the internationally renowned Great Gable, is in truth a worthy fell in its own right: its status is not diminished by the imposing presence of big brother, but merely by its own inability to assert itself more effectively above the aptly named divide of Windy Gap. Green Gable's little summit is a pleasant, lofty perch, and diverting eyes from Gable Crag it has much else to offer. The fell is of sufficient altitude to add the delights of the Buttermere Valley to what is probably the most complete view of Ennerdale's upper miles, watched over by an impressive Pillar. Well below Green Gable's own humbler crags the old track of Moses' Trod traverses the tongue high above Ennerdale.

A five minute descent through dusty red scree has the slim defile of Windy Gap underfoot, during which time Styhead Tarn appears below. The ensuing pull onto Great Gable proves the roughest section of the walk, a rocky clamber above Gable Crag onto the stony summit dome. Easier strides cross the boulder-strewn felltop to one of Lakeland's favourite summits. On touching the highest rock, a final reward is the memorable appearance of Wastwater, set deep in its trench of fells and leading the eye to the Irish Sea.

A cairned path begins the descent by heading east, an easy stony course down to a mini rock gateway where the path swings briefly right across a shelf. An award-winning stone path takes over for the remainder of the long descent to Sty Head, replacing unstable slopes of eroded scree: in addition to protecting the mountain, the firmly set stones also afford a very easy passage. When Sty Head and its tarn appear they still seem a long way down, but the boulder and attendant stretcher box are soon reached as the path leads directly to the crest of the pass.

A mist-filled Buttermere Valley from the summit of Great Gable

Turning north the path runs past the shore of Styhead Tarn, a place to linger with the work all but done. A little downstream a footbridge is reached, giving a choice of finishes. The main path crosses and resumes downstream, dropping to Stockley Bridge then along the valley floor back to Seathwaite.

Of greater interest is the path remaining on the west bank, descending to the wooded environs of Taylorgill Force. The great plume of the falls is revealed from a super vantage point, and the path undertakes a spirited traverse across a scree slope beneath Base Brown's craggy flank. A brief hands-on section sees the path down to a gate, a final viewpoint for the falls. Easier going leads into pastures through which the path runs back to the farm at Seathwaite, ultimately alongside the youthful Derwent.

Left: Great Gable from Lingmell. The Great Napes are the main crags on the face of the mountain, while the Wasdale Head-Sty Head path is clearly visible across the lower slopes

Scafell Pike and Ill Crag from Sampson's Stones, Upper Eskdale

SCAFELL PIKE   3209ft/978m

England's loftiest mountain is, fittingly enough, probably its finest: only Great Gable could lay similar claim to the crown. To add to its list of credits, the Pike stands at the epicentre of the best of mountain Lakeland, surrounded by such loyal subjects as Bowfell, Scafell and Gable, and with the untamed wilderness of the upper Esk on one side and the deep void of Wasdale on the other. Here is a mountain that lives up to its reputation. There are no forgettable days on the Pike.

Only five other English peaks elevate themselves above the 3000-foot contour, and three of these are Scafell Pike's own entourage, Broad Crag, Ill Crag and Scafell, the latter having its own chapter. The other two are unsung, characterful tops that well meet the exacting demands of being part of England's highest acres, with rough, bouldery crests and steep and equally rough flanks.

Each top pulls to one side of the great ridge running from the Pike to Great End, with Broad Crag overlooking Lingmell and Piers Gill, and Ill Crag favourably sited above the upper fastnesses of the Esk. From many stations thereabouts its tapering lines form one of the finest mountain prospects. Both tops are within a stone's throw of the pulsating highway from Esk Hause to Scafell Pike, yet few of the hordes ever stray from their prescribed route, and Broad Crag and Ill Crag remain the preserve of the discerning fellwalker.

The roughnesses of Scafell Pike are legendary, the summit minefield of boulders being a natural obstacle course. The country's highest ground is celebrated by a solid stone platform, with steps built in to enable zealous visitors to steal a few artificial feet. The unparalleled glut of building materials has been put to further use to construct a range of shelters, those to the east of the summit resembling miniature sheepfolds. Scafell Pike's greatest natural features are Pikes Crag, which includes Pulpit Rock, and the hidden cliff of Dow Crag (better known as Esk Buttress) on the little explored Eskdale flank. With Scafell it shares the unique saddle of Mickledore, a narrow, short-lived ridge that links the mountains while effectively denying access to Scafell. Cause of this impasse is Scafell Crag, a masterpiece of rock architecture seen to good advantage from the northern end of Mickledore.

Almost all ascents emanate from Borrowdale or Wasdale Head. While the latter provides the quicker ascents, Seathwaite in Borrowdale has the twin advantages of greater accessibility and a beautiful approach by Stockley Bridge and Styhead Tarn. Perhaps the finest route, equally practicable from either start point, involves an ascent from Sty Head of Great End's Band, then adding Ill Crag and Broad Crag to the high-level march. The extra climbing over Great End can be avoided by a more circuitous trail from Sty Head round to Esk Hause: from Seathwaite this is more directly reached by way of Grains Gill.

Other well tramped approaches to Esk Hause are from Great Langdale by way of Rossett Gill and Angle Tarn, and from Stonethwaite by way of the long miles of Langstrath. Sty Head is also a launch pad for the Corridor Route. This classic ascent line traverses the flanks of Great End and Broad Crag, linking the Lingmell col with Sty Head, and is a famous promenade for taking in the striking scenery between Lingmell and Great End.

Ascents from Wasdale Head need not first proceed to Sty Head: one route sets out for it but turns south for an absorbing climb alongside the ravine of Piers Gill, to then reach the summit either by the Lingmell or Broad Crag cols. The most direct ascent from the hamlet makes for Lingmell Gill, also reached from the campsite at the head of Wastwater. While one branch ascends over the broad western ridge of Lingmell, the main route climbs Brown Tongue into Hollow Stones: options go either side of Pikes Crag, the southern route first ascending roughly to Mickledore.

The only way to avoid the crowds is to start from Eskdale. The rewards are incalculable, early miles by the effervescent Esk leading to Lakeland's greatest wilderness in the amphitheatre of Great Moss. A path continues all the way to Esk Hause, but the usual route is a clamber up by the delights of Cam Spout to Mickledore: also on offer is the less frequented Little Narrowcove a little further north.

A rough lane leaves the green, passing the church which can also be reached by fieldpath from the hamlet. The walled lane runs to Burnthwaite, and from the outset enjoys superb views of this mountain surround, with the Pillar group to the left, Kirk Fell and Great Gable in front, Great End and Lingmell to the right, and back to Illgill Head and Wastwater. Beyond the farm a broad track runs through emerald pastureland between widely spaced walls.

Emerging by the wide stony bed of Lingmell Beck, the way runs on to a footbridge on inflowing Gable Beck, where a branch climbs left towards Great Gable. Two minutes further it reaches a less obvious fork. While the main arm rises across Gable's flank, a

fainter way keeps faith with the beck. This is an easy stroll into the heart of the mountains, with Great End now more dominant ahead and the Great Napes on Gable towering above. A few cairns guide the way across a series of side-streams to approach the confluence of Spouthead Gill and Piers Gill under Lingmell. Around this point Broad Crag briefly shows itself, tantalisingly high beyond the dark turrets above Piers Gill.

The path crosses Spouthead Gill a hundred yards above the confluence, and zigzags up a grassy tongue in between. As Piers Gill swings off right, the main path continues its grassy zigzags, re-crossing the southern arm of Spouthead Gill and then on up to cross its northern arm into a green bowl. A line of cairns in the lush turf send a path right, but this rises to the Corridor Route beneath the great gash of Skew Gill: instead another path bears left before rising to emerge onto Sty Head. The summit of the pass is marked by a massive boulder and a stretcher box at a junction of popular paths. Styhead Tarn appears just as the crest is gained.

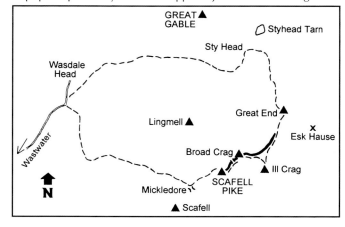

While Great Gable rises north-west of the pass, the steep slopes of Great End hover to the south-east: this hoary fell forms an abrupt northern buttress to the highest ridgeline in England. At Sty Head a right turn takes the broad path bound for Esk Hause, with the bony rib of the Band tumbling from the summit plateau of Great End directly ahead, a natural and rewarding stairway. Whilst a very faint path breaks off the Esk Hause path just before crossing the parallel beck, the purist's route involves tackling the Band immediately, outflanking small outcrops before a tiny saddle marks the arrival of the aforementioned path.

The path takes a clear line up the Band, pausing at a trough above the start of the ravine of Skew Gill. Above this point the going roughens a little, hardly surprising in view of the intimidating slopes above. The main path finds an easier way to the right of an early little scramble, then any number of ways can be picked through the boulders, with easy optional scrambles to the right of the path: on becoming steeper and stonier, a bouldery option to its right becomes increasingly irresistible.

The drama culminates on a slabby platform, where the well worn path climbs from the left. A gentler rise leads onto the north-west cairn, which with its adjacent shelter makes a splendid viewpoint for Wasdale and Great Gable. Also greeting the eye is the high, bouldery ridge of Scafell Pike and its trusty satellites Ill Crag and Broad Crag. Despite being little over 200 feet superior, England's premier mountain still succeeds in appearing monstrous.

Across a minor depression on this broad top waits the slightly higher summit cairn. En route, the dramatic upper reaches of a sombre network of cliffs and gullies can be inspected, with an aerial view of Sprinkling Tarn leading the eye into Borrowdale; finest feature is the rift of Central Gully, a popular winter ascent route (for the experienced and equipped) which gains the plateau just yards short of the summit. New aspects of the view eastwards include the Langdale Pikes and the long Helvellyn skyline.

Walkers leaving Scafell Pike's summit for Wasdale: Pillar and the Mosedale Horseshoe ahead, with Kirk Fell in front of High Stile

In the saddle on Great End's plateau a cairned path gently drops to meet the Esk Hause-Scafell Pike path at the Calf Cove col. After a stony climb onto the shoulder of Ill Crag, easier going tempts a detour south to Ill Crag's summit. This will guarantee further solitude and some stunning views into the unfrequented haven of upper Eskdale, with a lower top perched even more dramatically above the valley head. This is also a first-class vantage point for appraising the position of Broad Crag in relation to the massif.

From Ill Crag the main path is rejoined in the Ill Crag col, and after a slight rise across Broad Crag's shoulder, devotees of rough ground will revel in the briefest of detours onto surely the roughest mountain summit in Lakeland. A neat cairn occupies the highest of the massive boulders on this remarkable top. A little caution ensures an even shorter drop back onto the path, with the final saddle, the Broad Crag col, below. The final climb starts rough and stony, and ends by crossing the bouldery uppermost slopes of England's highest acres to gain the mighty platform that rises above all else. An Ordnance Survey column cowers a few steps away.

So often in shadow when viewed from Scafell Pike is the craggy face of Scafell to the south-west, and the next objective, also in view, is the narrow, connecting ridge of Mickledore. The main cairned way heads west off the summit, but within 200 yards a profusely cairned junction sends a slightly less obvious branch left. In poor visibility it is better to stay on the 'tourist' path down towards the Lingmell col, swinging left just before it to drop down towards Brown Tongue.

For Mickledore, the left branch descends steadily to this short-lived ridge abutting onto the no-go area of the mighty Scafell Crag. While famous features such as Broad Stand and Lord's Rake can be identified, it is the sheer might of the crag itself that will be remembered. The presence of a stretcher box is sufficient warning that in this vicinity there are more situations than usual in which to come unstuck.

In the very nick a massive cairn sends a rough path down the Wasdale side, and the wall of Pulpit Rock on Pikes Crag enters the scene to the right. As the path quickly opens out, zigzags make life easier until being deposited into the grassy amphitheatre of Hollow Stones. A lengthy pause is merited to savour the atmosphere of this rock-walled prison, with both Scafell Crag and Pikes Crag hovering menacingly above.

As the path resumes, the direct descent path merges in from the right amid relaxing, grassy surrounds. Merging with a side-stream, the superbly built path shadows it down beneath the spur of Brown Tongue to a confluence with Lingmell Gill. Crossing in this charming setting, the lively stream leads down to a kissing-gate through which a contouring path branches right. This gains the base of Lingmell's west ridge and provides a splendid moment as the Wasdale Head scene returns ahead, the hamlet backed as ever by Pillar. The path makes an easy-angled slant down to a footbridge on Lingmell Beck, and across the pasture the road is joined just a minute short of the green.

CONISTON OLD MAN 2634ft/803m

The Old Man of Coniston is one of Lakeland's favourite characters, and shares with Helvellyn and Skiddaw an attraction for visitors unaccustomed to the high tops. No other Lake District mountain has endured such an all-round onslaught at the hands of man: the lower slopes bear fascinating evidence of copper mining activity, absorbing industrial relics overshadowed by the higher altitude slate quarries. Such is the resilience of the mountain that it can shrug off such blemishes and still project an endearing front.

Almost all ascents of the Old Man begin from the village it shelters: there are numerous ways of tackling the rough flanks, and none lack interest. The finest introduction - and the gentlest start - involves a walk through Coppermines Valley, as the valley of Levers Water Beck is commonly known. Behind the superbly sited youth hostel a climb to Boulder Valley precedes a scramble that emerges dramatically on the shore of Low Water; here the pulsating artery of the popular route from Miners Bridge is joined for the final zigzags. The normal route climbs more directly through old quarry workings to Low Water.

Several means of avoiding the main highway to the top involve the Walna Scar Pass. Surfaced on leaving the village, a wide track on gaining the open fell, and ultimately a fine walkers' path as it heads for the watershed with the Duddon Valley, it can be vacated at either Boo Tarn for a real zigzag of a climb, or at the entrance to The Cove, then either scaling the broad south ridge or preferably entering the Cove to pass Goat's Water and enjoy a dramatic picture of the mighty cliffs of Dow Crag. This circuitous course then climbs to Goat's Hause before doubling back to the top. By continuing to the top of Walna Scar Pass, a fine walk over Dow Crag can be enjoyed before descending to Goat's Hause.

Wetherlam from Swirl How

The Old Man's crown is unmistakeable, for it supports an immense slate platform which itself bears a cairn. The whole is perched above the steep eastern face, and the bird's-eye prospect of Low Water is one of Lakeland's finest. If looking elsewhere one cannot fail to be impressed by the two-sided picture. Inland rise the hills, a continuous line-up of summits rather than a balanced mountain scene; the southern arc depicts the decreasing foothills of southern Lakeland, intermingled with various lakes and tarns and culminating in an extensive coastline formed by the many indentations of Morecambe Bay.

The tight-knit group of Coniston Fells is largely detached from its neighbours, the only link with higher ground being at 1289ft/393m on Wrynose Pass. In truth the principal summit of the Coniston Fells is Swirl How, for despite being marginally overtopped by the Old Man, this peak sends ridges radiating to all points of the compass. The minor top of Great Carrs shares the

head of the Greenburn Valley with Swirl How, while further west the least frequented of the group, Grey Friar overlooks the upper miles of the Duddon Valley. These northern summits are easily accessible from Little Langdale, where Wet Side Edge offers an easy-angled staircase.

Wetherlam stands aloof to the east of Swirl How, linked by the pass of Swirl Hause and the ridge of Prison Band. It is more often climbed in its own right than any of the others, for it enjoys a superb location watching over the delectable low country around Tilberthwaite, and has its own fine ascent ridge in Wetherlam Edge. Dow Crag is another fell of the Duddon, though its prized asset is its eponymous cliff face, which looks across Goat's Water to the Old Man: it also boasts the finest summit of the group.

ROUTE 8: CONISTON OLD MAN

Summits:
Coniston Old Man   2634ft/803m
Swirl How   2631ft/802m
Wetherlam   2503ft/763m

Start: *Coniston (SD 302975). Central car park. Buses from Ambleside and Ulverston.*

Distance: *8½ miles/13½km*   **Ascent:** *3400ft/1036m*

Maps:
OS 1:50,000 - Landranger 89 or 90 and 96 or 97
1:25,000 - Outdoor Leisure 6

A narrow road leaves the village centre on the south side of the bridge on Church Beck. Climbing to the Sun Hotel, a short-lived lane runs behind it to a gate at the last buildings. A broad track runs through the field, crossing a sidestream just above its confluence with Church Beck, then climbing above the main beck's

Great How Crags on Swirl How, from the Coppermines Valley

The slate path rises to a fork, with a dark tunnel to the left beneath a prostrate cable stanchion. Bearing right to rise past the main quarry face and leave the site, a few steady minutes bring the path to the basin of Low Water. This is an inspirationally sited mountain tarn, with the summit ridge brooding directly above. The final stage sees the path rising left, engaging a fine series of zigzags up to yet higher-level quarry evidence. These smaller scale workings are negotiated to reach more open ground, and the path treads easier terrain for the final few minutes to the immense slate platform marking the summit of Coniston Old Man.

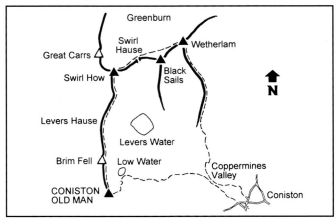

wooded environs. As the going eases the track passes fine water-falls to reach Miners Bridge. A path continues upstream to a gate, a stunning moment as the greater part of the walk shows itself, an imposing skyline running from the Old Man towards Swirl How. In front, the youth hostel in Coppermines Valley is prominent.

The path makes gentle progress to a wall corner at the top, with a final wall behind. The path rises onto an old quarry road, and turning right for a matter of yards to a fork, the left branch spirals steeply up to an extensive former quarry site. Looking back, Coniston Water is fully revealed, while beyond the coppermines are the pass of Swirl Hause and the peaks of Black Sails and Wetherlam. Two sets of ruins are encountered, featuring stone sheds, rusting cables and tramway tracks in amongst the spoilheaps.

From the Old Man long strides are the order of the day, northwards along the rim of Low Water's comb, with a broad path on excellent turf leading to the solid cairn on Brim Fell. Little more than a stepping-stone between the two major tops, Brim Fell holds the dubious distinction of being the least interesting summit in this group of hills. A visit to the eastern slopes is repaid with a striking view down into the heart of the copper mining district; here its rugged east face can be seen to conform to the general pattern of the group.

Advancing along the whaleback ridge the saddle of Levers Hause interrupts the climb to Swirl How. From this vicinity there are good views over Levers Water to Coniston village and lake. The short climb to Swirl How is interrupted by the modest tops of Little How Crags and Great How Crags, which in mist are wrongly assumed to be Swirl How's top. Swirl How's cairn appears just two minutes before gaining it across a tilted, stony plateau, and reaching all of seven feet into the sky, it appears to teeter on the brink of an unbroken plunge to the Greenburn Valley. This is a grand place to savour the atmosphere of the Lakeland Fells.

Within yards of the cairn a splendid descent of the east ridge, Prison Band, begins. This melodramatic name has induced writers to far exaggerate its nature, and while a heady mountain atmosphere pervades, the path encounters nothing more than an occasional rock step. Ahead, Wetherlam initially appears subdued, yet as height is lost its inclusion in the route can seem a more daunting prospect. At the base of the ridge the pass of Swirl Hause is reached, from where a quicker return descends a path to Levers Water for the upper Coppermines Valley. The main path climbs away to the east, soon easing to traverse across the northern slopes of Black Sails (a summit worth detouring onto) to climb onto Wetherlam's summit, where the cairn occupies a rocky knoll on a small plateau.

Wetherlam's detachment from the Coniston group permits views of a very different nature. To the north the great mountain barriers of the Scafells, Bowfell and Helvellyn are majestically ranged, with the adjacent Coniston Fells forming a solid wall with their impressive eastern faces. At its feet, however, is what makes Wetherlam special, the contrasting low country stretching from Tilberthwaite over to Windermere. Intermittently lavishly wooded

Coniston Old Man in Alpine raiment on an Easter weekend

and bracken-covered foothills, dappled with plentiful sheets of water culminating in England's largest lake, ensure an altogether memorable landscape.

South of the summit, a large cairn is passed as a path quickly forms to runs above a couple of airy drops towards Dry Cove Moss. It then ambles down the broad ridge of Lad Stones, with Coniston Water ahead. The walking is exceptionally easy as the path runs down, savouring a splendid array of Coniston's rugged fells on the right, with Levers Water appearing beneath them. Unexpectedly the path swings left off the ridge to avoid steeper ground ahead, with the old quarrymans' path evident below, along the edge of Yewdale Moss. The path becomes occasionally faint, but descends pleasantly to join the old way at Hole Rake above a steep drop to the Coppermines Valley.

The path turns to work down into the valley behind a row of former miners' cottages, whose track joins the level mine road. Passing Miners Bridge en route, this rough road drops down above some lively scenery as Church Beck tumbles in fine waterfalls through a deep gorge. On acquiring a surface the road runs back into the village alongside the Black Bull.

HIGH RAISE   2500ft/762m

The hub of Lakeland is High Raise's claim to fame, though the felltop holds few delights for the walker. Its broad, featureless summit acres do however crown a particularly extensive network of valleys and ridges, with the celebrated Langdale Pikes and the more lowly yet spectacular outlines of Eagle Crag and Tarn Crag among its portfolio. These distinctive tops attract walkers from the valleys immediately below, namely Borrowdale, Langdale and Easedale, while High Raise watches from a position of anonymity.

On the summit an Ordnance Survey column presides over the rash of High White Stones. This being the highest point of the central fells it could not fail to command a first-rate panorama, indeed it is a challenge to detect the omission of any notable heights. The nearest superior ground is south-west, where the high peaks of the Scafell group stand shoulder to shoulder beyond the trough of Stake Pass.

Key to direct ascents is the lofty pass of Greenup Edge linking Borrowdale with Grasmere, giving enjoyable climbs from the former via Greenup Gill or Eagle Crag, or the latter via Far Easedale, Tarn Crag or the Helm Crag ridge. Above Great Langdale, High Raise is stubbornly defended by the Langdale Pikes, inferior in height and little else. Most ascents from this side incorporate one or more of the Pikes, though a direct route onto High Raise can be steered between them into Harrison Combe, or by way of Stickle Tarn and the shapely eminence of Sergeant Man.

Harrison Stickle is highest of the celebrated Langdale Pikes, and most prominent in the scores of classic viewpoints in and beyond Great Langdale. The one realistic start point of Dungeon Ghyll offers a plethora of well trodden routes. A direct path via Pike How stays well above the ravines of Dungeon Ghyll for a remarkably easy walk up into the hollow of Harrison Combe, with a stiff pull to conclude. An equally popular route breasts Loft Crag's flanks, though is rougher in its upper reaches before entering the combe between Loft Crag and Thorn Crag.

Entirely different in character are approaches via Stickle Gill. A clambering path shadows this lively beck to its source in Stickle Tarn, conferring the benefits of a close look at the mighty cliff of Pavey Ark. Though a worn path climbs between Harrison Stickle and Pavey Ark, the finest route of all is a scramble across the tilted Jack's Rake, which strikes an audacious course across the crag. In truth it is a straightforward if sustained scramble, surprisingly well protected from exposure, for the most part, by a low outer wall.

ROUTE 9: HIGH RAISE

Summits:
High Raise   2500ft/762m
Harrison Stickle   2415ft/736m
Pike o'Stickle   2326ft/709m

Start: Dungeon Ghyll (NY 295064). The New Hotel is half a mile short of the B5343's end at the Old Hotel. National Park and National Trust car parks. Served by bus from Ambleside.

Distance: 6½ miles/10½km   **Ascent:** 2762ft/842m

Maps:
OS 1:50,000 - Landranger 89 or 90. 1:25,000 - Outdoor Leisure 6

Entirely hidden by the bold front of the Langdale Pikes, High Raise exerts no influence on Dungeon Ghyll, and indeed only becomes relevant late in the ascent. From the drive to the New Hotel, a gate by the side of a cottage sends a path up a wallside and into an enclosure behind. Rising between small clusters of trees the path runs alongside Stickle Gill, soon crossing it at a footbridge. Upstream the path passes through an old sheepfold, and at the next sidestream a lesser but clear path doubles back uphill, giving a splendid ascent on delightful zigzags.

Half way up the path forks, and the left branch is ignored in favour of the grassy zigzags. The peak of Harrison Stickle soars across Stickle Gill, and the path remains a gem all the way up to a crumbling enclosure. Improving views look back over the valley to the Coniston Fells and around to Crinkle Crags at the dalehead.

Passing a ruin, the zigzags fade as the path climbs a grassy tongue. Higher again, the increasingly faint path slants away from the adjacent gill as it runs above a sidestream onto easier ground. Now very faint, all is made clear as the rocky dome of Sergeant Man appears. It is dramatically followed by the magnificent cliff of Pavey Ark, straight in front, and within seconds Harrison Stickle joins it. Advancing in the direction of Sergeant Man a clear, level path is met as Stickle Tarn appears over to the left.

Turning away from the drama, a short level stroll sees the path climb through a stony area. Cairns indicate an early fork, the left branch passing a ruined shelter to become faint. Turning to scale inviting grassy slopes between low rock outcrops, occasional cairns aid progress as the path gains the ridge descending from Sergeant Man, and dividing Langdale from Easedale. Ahead is the long skyline of the Fairfield Horseshoe and the Ill Bell ridge, and behind is the classic view of Stickle Tarn and its guardian peaks.

The thin path meanders amiably along, and the Helvellyn massif appears at a small pool in a dip in the ridge. A few yards further, cairns confirm the presence of the main ridge path, and just ahead, the well worn Easedale path also gains the ridge. A choice of paths set forth up the knobbly ridge, the northerly (Easedale) one better promoted by cairns. As height is gained the peak of Sergeant Man beckons more closely, and on closing in it is revealed in its true colours as a marvellous sham, as near-level ground is seen behind it.

The path curves around to the rocky top, a grand place to be. This shapely peak is a notable landmark in distant views, and a neat cairn looks down over Bright Beck to the arresting profile of Pavey Ark above Stickle Tarn. The least interesting part of the view is north-west to High Raise, and of several paths radiating away, the main one crosses rougher ground before a gentle rise to the summit. A line of forlorn fenceposts provide temporary company, but 200 yards short of the top they leave the path to forge straight on to gain the OS column and shelter on the rash of stones.

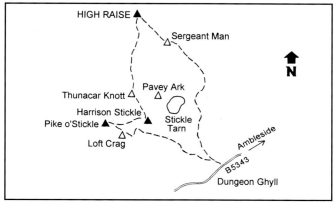

A good path departs south, bound for the Langdale Pikes which are currently overtopped by the Coniston Fells, while to the right is majestic Bowfell. A long decline leads to a saddle at the head of Bright Beck, and straight up the facing slope is the gently domed top of Thunacar Knott. A sturdy cairn is passed as the path runs on by the summit cairn. Now its illustrious neighbours the Langdale Pikes are little more than a stone's throw away, yet still curiously insignificant from behind the scenes.

Loft Crag from Pike o'Stickle, featuring Gimmer Crag with Windermere, Lingmoor Fell and Blea Tarn beyond

While the main path declines over easy ground into the basin of Harrison Combe, the route to Harrison Stickle leaves Thunacar Knott's cairn by a choice of thinner paths south-east, bound for the saddle in front of a rock tor before Harrison Stickle. Near two pools a clearer path comes in from Pavey Ark, and runs on to another saddle just under Harrison Stickle's summit, with a two-minute climb to the cairn.

The summit lives up to the fell's general appeal, a bristly crown bedecked with shapely cairns. Crags guard the top to south and east, from where the most dramatic views are obtained. Three very different features earn a mention, the first being an aerial view of Langdale, its lush green floor curving away towards Windermere; next is a side-on picture of Pavey Ark hovering above Stickle Tarn; and third an outstanding line-up of peaks hemming in the valley head.

Most inviting aspect is the shapely nipple of Pike o'Stickle. Retracing steps to the minor saddle between the summit and the rock tor to the north, a path junction sends a branch left, descending easy ground to meet another path in the amphitheatre of Harrison Combe. Across the stream the path aims directly for Pike o'Stickle, rising to the head of a great scree shoot where Neolithic man worked stone axe 'factories'. The scree run was at one time a Lakeland classic, though its popularity has seen it 'run out', and it is firmly not recommended as a descent route.

Pike o'Stickle's graceful cone thrusts itself skyward from the mass of the mountainside and the barricade of cliffs wrapped around it, and the final climb is as exhilarating as one cares to make it: the normal route climbs to the right before clambering back up the rocky top. Arrival on the neat top is equally exciting, being greeted by an airiness seldom experienced on a Lakeland summit. This is a place to soak up atmosphere, while lapping up two outstanding examples of mountain architecture supplied by Gimmer Crag on neighbouring Loft Crag, and Bowfell asserting its full height from Mickleden to summit cairn, an exalted profile.

From the base of the summit cone the path skirting the head of the scree run is retraced before continuing over gentle knolls onto Loft Crag. This third of the Langdale Pikes is a less famous cousin of the Stickle brothers, which are displayed better from here than from any other single vantage point. It also boasts one of Langdale's best known cliffs and a charming summit. The rockface in question is Gimmer Crag, a climbers' favourite that falls away only a short distance below the very summit, which is itself a tiny perch high above the plunge into Mickleden.

Advancing east along the short crest, the path drops left onto easier ground, or from the very end a downward scramble is needed to reach the grassy knoll below. Just a couple of minutes further a large cairn in the lowest point marks a path junction, with the cairned top of Thorn Crag in front. The left branch crosses

Pike o'Stickle from Loft Crag, backed by Great End and Great Gable

the stream of Dungeon Ghyll, now almost at the neck of the combe, alongside the rapidly forming ravines of Dungeon Ghyll.

A broad path is joined just across the stream, to enjoy an exit from the combe by airily traversing a narrow defile above the upper falls of the ravine. Beneath the summit stack of Harrison Stickle the path slants down contrastingly genteel slopes. Ahead are the waters of Windermere, Elterwater, Blea Tarn and more distantly Morecambe Bay.

During this stage Dungeon Ghyll is revealed, with grand waterfalls and ravine scenery of the highest order: looking back, the summit of Harrison Stickle appears as a noble peak, with the rugged Thorn Crag to its left. The path descends a steeply winding course beneath the rocky bluff of Pike How, then down by a wall above the calmer lower reaches of the beck. The wall leads down to a kissing-gate above the enclosure where the walk began.

HELVELLYN 3117ft/950m

Helvellyn is the highest mountain in England outside of the Scafells, it is the most frequently climbed Lakeland peak, and in Striding Edge it boasts the most famous ridge on any English mountain.

Helvellyn surmounts Lakeland's loftiest mountain wall, a mighty north-south ridge effectively splitting the district in two. To the west, slopes fall in uniform drabness to the afforested environs of Thirlmere, ease of access from the Ambleside-Keswick road being the reason for so many dull ascents therefrom. Most popular are routes from the car parks at Wythburn and Swirls, south of Thirlspot.

Interest on the Wythburn route is found by branching off onto Nethermost Pike to finish along the scarp above Striding Edge. Paths from Swirls and Thirlspot both make for the skyline crest of Browncove Crags, while a bridleway from Thirlspot joins the ridge further north, on White Side. Further north again, the summit of Sticks Pass, reached either from Legburthwaite or Glenridding via Greenside by way of a time-honoured packhorse route, offers a high-level approach over the summits of Raise and White Side.

To the east, Helvellyn could not present a more different aspect. Striding Edge and Swirral Edge break boldly away from the mountain, their arms enfolding Red Tarn, which reflects the hill's sombre face directly below the summit. Striding Edge is a legendary character, with an inspiring name to quicken the pulse. While in terms of obligatory scrambling and degrees of exposure it is put to shame by countless Scottish summit ridges, it is nevertheless an exciting place to be. The only time for concern should be if unexpectedly fierce winds arise; in winter conditions it is obviously the preserve of the experienced and well equipped mountain walker.

Striding Edge can be gained either from Patterdale or Glenridding. From the former, a path climbs from the entrance to Grisedale onto the ridge at the celebrated 'Hole in the Wall'. This can be reached from Glenridding either via Greenside and Red Tarn Beck, or more directly via Mires Beck onto Birkhouse Moor. For the most part the well trodden path runs below the actual crest, though the sporting regularly attempt the purists' way. Only at one point, almost at the very end are all limbs required to be used in earnest; even then it is a sheltered scramble with little sense of exposure, and with a lengthy alternative to circumvent it.

While the final climb up to Helvellyn's summit from the end of Striding Edge is a slithery, eroded scramble, the equivalent pull on Swirral Edge is far superior, being a steep clamber up solid, easily gripped rock virtually onto the very summit: its only failing is that it doesn't last long enough. If approaching from Glenridding it is more logical to ascend via Swirral Edge and then return over Striding Edge; even from Patterdale, Swirral Edge is easily gained by a contouring path from the Hole in the Wall to Red Tarn.

Two other well trodden routes from the east are via the Keppel Cove zigzags from Glenridding and the more circuitous Grisedale from Patterdale, via Grisedale Tarn and the zigzags of Dollywaggon Pike. Each option is far better as a return route after ascending by one of the edges. Helvellyn's closest supporting tops can be used as inviting stepping-stones, notably Catstycam, reached by a branch off the Keppel Cove path; and also Nethermost Pike and Dollywaggon Pike to the south, each of which has interesting routes up their eastern ridge from the upper reaches of Grisedale.

After the delights of its two edges, Helvellyn's summit is a distinct anti-climax, being broad, grassy, and lacking even a worthwhile cairn: a stone shelter does a roaring trade with foraging sheep attracted to the contents of sandwich boxes. A little further south a

Left: looking back to Catstycam from Birkhouse Moor

tablet commemorates the landing of an aeroplane, while more romantically, the Gough Memorial above the start of Striding Edge pays tribute to the remarkable faithfulness of a dog that remained with its owner's body for three months, causing both Wordsworth and Scott to pen moving lines. Though its two famous edges draw most attention, a contributory factor to Helvellyn's popularity is its reputation as a viewpoint. The immense void of central Lakeland ensures the various mountain groups of the district are beheld from a well proportioned distance.

ROUTE 10: HELVELLYN

Summits:
Catstycam   2920ft/890m
Helvellyn   3117ft/950m

Start: *Glenridding (NY 386169). Central car park. Served by Patterdale-Penrith buses, and seasonal services from Bowness and Keswick.*

Distance: 8 miles/13km   **Ascent:** 3000ft/914m

Maps:
OS 1:50,000 - Landranger 90. 1:25,000 - Outdoor Leisure 5

Glenridding is left by a side road alongside the beck from the shops, narrowing to a path and passing a campsite to reach Rattlebeck Bridge. An access road rises left to Miresbeck, but the route quickly forks right over a side beck on the track climbing above the house. Continuing straight up at a fork, a right turn in front of a small wood sees a stony path climb to a stile onto the open fell.

Shunning the path climbing by the beck, a path heads right for a long, near-level mile under Birkhouse Moor, with Sheffield Pike rising out of the devastation of the old Greenside lead mines across Glenridding Beck. Rounding a corner the path rises to a higher level path on the course of a former water leat opposite the upper buildings at Greenside. The environs of the mine workings are quickly left behind, and the lively beck is rejoined at a footbridge above a small dam.

Catstycam can be omitted by remaining on the south side of the beck, a lengthy stride preceding a climb on its other bank to just short of Red Tarn, from where a path rises to gain the saddle on Swirral Edge linking Catstycam with Helvellyn. The full route crosses the bridge, and a lower track and a stony clamber lead up to a higher stony track rising away from the buildings. A fork sees the main track commence a splendid course above Red Tarn Beck, beneath scrubby, juniper-clad flanks. Rising only gently, proceedings are entirely dominated by the fine peak of Catstycam.

Further on, a branch right sees the old pony track take off for the Helvellyn ridge, but the onward route runs on to approach Keppel Cove's concrete dam. Ahead are Lower Man and White Side,

The Helvellyn group from Place Fell, across Ullswater

while the ascent route is seen in profile. Walkers are warned they cross the breached dam at their own risk: the alternative way is to remain on the track to a sheepfold where a thin path takes over, past a breached upper embankment and some ruins from where an old water cut runs on to the beck. Across, grassy slopes rise to the base of Catstycam's north-east ridge.

Despite its appearance from certain vantage points, the ridge is ill defined at the outset, but slanting left a clear path is joined. As this winds unerringly up, the going improves on the tapering upper contours. The last section is a firmer path on easier ground, gaining the summit cairn with a sense of disbelief. The reward is a spectacular picture of the glistening waters of Red Tarn, backed by Striding Edge and the mighty eastern face of Helvellyn. If Helvellyn is the king of its own group, then Catstycam is its queen, a slender peak with that rare gift of good looks from every direction.

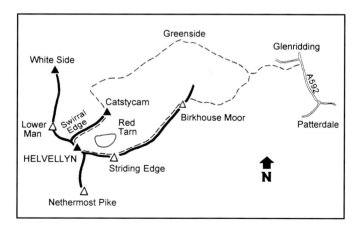

From Catstycam's airy perch a rapid descent is made to the saddle preceding the dramatic course of Swirral Edge. A near-level walk leads to the base of the steep section to commence an exhilarating confrontation. Although far shorter than its illustrious counterpart across the tarn, Swirral Edge has the advantage of a more solid rock scramble to attain the summit plateau. Those averse to employing hands can weave to either side of the arete proper, and the whole episode should only encounter potential danger in winter conditions or very strong winds. From the cairned top a broad path runs south above the escarpment to the OS column, a little beyond which is the lacklustre summit cairn and, below that, a well patronised shelter.

The return by way of Striding Edge is a truly classic route, but in poor conditions alternative descents might be advisable. These include the broad bridleway southwards over Dollywaggon Pike to Grisedale Tarn, or north over White Side to the Keppel Cove zigzags.

From Helvellyn's summit the way lies south, preferably following the rim of the eastern face to the Gough Memorial of 1890. The roughest part of the walk then sees the path clamber ungainly down stony, eroded slopes before gaining the edge. A slabby finale with good holds leads down onto the saddle, a neat defile where Striding Edge proper begins. At once the only true scramble presents itself, a short climb up a chimney with a wealth of holds. Those unnerved by this have formed a broad escape path around to the right. Atop this clamber, one can opt to cling rigidly to the spiked crest, or take to a parallel path running a few feet below on the north side.

Visited by relatively few is the edge's highest point on High Spying How, while firmly affixed to the crest nearby is the Dixon Memorial, erected in 1858 in memory of a follower of the Patterdale Foxhounds who fell to his doom. As the edge diminishes in grandeur, walkers gradually resort to this path, and gently declining

Looking down onto Striding Edge from Helvellyn

ground leads to a stile at the Hole in the Wall. The Patterdale path crosses here, but the Glenridding route advances along the ridge to Birkhouse Moor, the natural continuation of Striding Edge.

The highest point of Birkhouse Moor is a scrappy cairn passed before the wall turns away. At the wall-end a restored path quickly turns to commence the descent, with a possible diversion out to Birkhouse Moor's prominent north-east cairn. The main path swings down to meet the wall again, before winding away from it to a circular fold. Here a steeper descent spirals down in company with Mires Beck, with Glenridding and the glorious scenery of Ullswater outspread below. Ultimately the path crosses the beck before rejoining the outward route at the base of the fell.

FAIRFIELD 2864ft/873m
SAINT SUNDAY CRAG 2759ft/841m

Often, in the crowded confines of Lakeland, elevated and important mountains occupy little space on the ground due to the near claustrophobic presence of subsidiary fells. Such is Fairfield, the major top in a neatly defined group to the south of Grisedale Hause. Ridges fanning out from the summit permit numerous horseshoe walks pivoted on Fairfield, and by far the most popular is that bearing Fairfield's name, based on Rydal. This circuit above the valley of Rydal Beck tramps the grassy south ridge over Heron Pike and Great Rigg, and the more interesting ridge initially heading eastwards onto Hart Crag and thence to Dove Crag. The south ridge can also be gained from Grasmere by a steep clamber onto Stone Arthur, from where a gentler path rises to Great Rigg.

More rewarding is a circuit of Deepdale from Patterdale, for Fairfield's grandest face is then revealed in all its glory, with the bonus of a traverse of its classiest ridge onto Saint Sunday Crag: a highlight is the crossing of the miniature peak of Cofa Pike, a short distance from Fairfield's summit. Deepdale Hause, between Fairfield and Saint Sunday Crag, can be gained by a path along the floor of Deepdale climbing steeply to the pass; and also more easily from the outflow of Grisedale Tarn, reached from Patterdale, Grasmere or Dunmail Raise. Of all approaches to Fairfield, only the direct haul from Grisedale Hause cannot be recommended, consisting of little short of a thousand feet of unremitting collarwork.

The summit of the fell is an interesting place to be, and in bad weather a confusing one, with an absence of paths on the stony plateau. Only yards from the shelter the plateau meets an abrupt demise at the onset of the long wall of crags lining the head of Deepdale. As a viewpoint Fairfield ranks favourably, with an unbroken western skyline beyond miles of lower ground, a striking line-up of the Helvellyn range from a satisfying angle, and an extensive picture of the High Street group.

Saint Sunday Crag from Hart Crag

Saint Sunday Crag is a graceful fell, and though really part of the Fairfield group, it is generally seen as a loner. Tapering at its south-western end to link with Fairfield at Deepdale Hause, the fell broadens during an undemanding and highly enjoyable climb to the summit. A steep, well defined ridge commences on the subsidiary top of Gavel Pike, to the east, while the main ridge continues in a north-easterly line, descending in stages to Patterdale. On the way its fall is broken by the lesser top of Birks.

Descending east from Hart Crag, with High Street and its many ridges and tops beyond Hartsop

Saint Sunday Crag is enclosed by Deepdale and Grisedale, and to the latter it presents a formidable line of crags presiding over an unrelenting mountain wall. This flank attracts a number of adventurers seeking a thrilling route to the top, for contained within the craggy confines are several gullies and rock scrambles, best known being Pinnacle Ridge. Most walkers content themselves with the traditional approach from Patterdale, commencing through the beautiful trees of Glenamara Park. Zigzags onto the spur of Thornhow End give way to more gentle gradients before the final section up the north-east ridge. Another fine way to the top is to reach Deepdale Hause from the foot of Grisedale Tarn, by means of a pleasurable path that effortlessly traverses the hillside.

While Saint Sunday Crag's top is plain, there are some splendid views to lap up. The most outstanding takes in Helvellyn and its supporters to the north-west, and irrepressible Ullswater to the north-east. In the case of the latter, it is really necessary to stroll in the direction of the lake to lose the rather drab foreground: only then is one of Lakeland's fairest prospects fully revealed.

51

Summits:
Saint Sunday Crag   2759ft/841m
Fairfield   2864ft/873m
Hart Crag   2697ft/822m

Start: *Patterdale (NY 395158). Village centre car park. Served by bus from Penrith, with seasonal services from Bowness and Keswick.*

Distance: *9½ miles/15km*   **Ascent:** *3172ft/967m*

Maps: *1:50,000 - Landranger 90. 1:25,000 - Outdoor Leisure 5*

A footpath sets off past the toilets opposite the phone box, on a track rising to a lone building. Behind it a thinner path turns left to run past Mill Moss to successive kissing-gates. Saint Sunday Crag's underling Birks hovers above, while Birkhouse Moor and Sheffield Pike rise to the right. The path runs through the open country of Glenamara Park, crossing Hag Beck en route. The views throughout this section are dominated by the beauty of Ullswater.

The path splits at a stile in the fence below, and the climb properly begins by turning up the ascending path. A steep pull through the odd trees gains the intake wall, which is crossed by a stile at its highest point on Thornhow End. Resuming uphill, the splendid path soon eases out to traverse across the flanks of Birks, high above Grisedale. With Saint Sunday Crag's upper reaches in front, the path runs on to a hause overlooking Gavel Moss at the base of the final climb. The main path makes a direct climb up the north-east ridge to jagged rocks at the top, and beyond this classic viewpoint it is but a few minutes' gentle rise to the summit cairn.

Heading off west, the ridge narrows to reveal better views into Deepdale, while the Helvellyn massif rears up across the deep gulf of Grisedale. There is a vast prospect westwards to Gable and the Scafells, and Grisedale Tarn nestles below. This easy stroll ends on Deepdale Hause, at the far end of which Fairfield's steep flanks await. This enjoyable clamber quickly gains the bristly eminence of Cofa Pike, whose crossing demands a steady hold for a few yards if traversing its true crest. Certainly it provides a lively if short-lived interlude before the final stony pull onto Fairfield's summit. The path falters on the broad top, and in poor conditions caution is needed in finding the main summit cairn (a shelter).

An improving, cairned path runs a good 100 yards south-east to round the head of a scree filled gully before striking east for Hart Crag. In clear weather the path might be vacated in order to appreciate the rugged scenery to the north, where innumerable vantage points overlook the cliffs and gullies around the head of Deepdale. The paths meet up after turning south to outcrops above Scrubby Crag, from where a short drop leads onto the neat defile of Link Hause. It is but a brief climb to Hart Crag, breaking off the main highway to gain one of the identical summits up to the right.

Hart Crag is an uncomplicated mountain, exhibiting much that is typical of Lakeland. Rough ground bounds the summit dome with its twin cairns, and all three paths thereto encounter bouldery slopes. Despite its stature Hart Crag is balked by the mass of its big brother across Link Hause, and several other nearby heights of similar altitude take up much of the panorama. To the west however Fairfield's south ridge is successfully overtopped to reveal a striking array of fells centred on the Scafell group.

Heading east from Hart Crag's north cairn, the ridge-path is crossed and a line of cairns guide a fledgling path downhill. Avoiding the north-eastern slopes, it declines gently before asserting itself on steeper ground. Equally assertive is the near vertical face of Dove Crag across to the right. The Hartsop above How ridge awaits below, and the path winds down onto easier ground. This is followed by a second, longer steep section which begins by being ushered right of a craggy knoll. Below, the path sets off along the broad, undulating ridge. There are outstanding views all around, with flanks falling roughly to the side valleys of Deepdale and Dovedale. A gentle rise leads to the minor summit of Hartsop above How, where nature has provided a well-angled backrest for viewing the triumvirate of Dove Crag, Hart Crag and Fairfield.

The gentle decline of this long, curving arm brings increasingly intimate views of the surroundings of Brotherswater and the Patterdale valley. A wall comes in for company but little else changes until scattered trees are entered towards the bottom. In deeper woodland the main path bears left, slanting down to a stile out into a field. A farm track in the centre leads down to a gate onto the main road at Bridgend, a mile south of Patterdale.

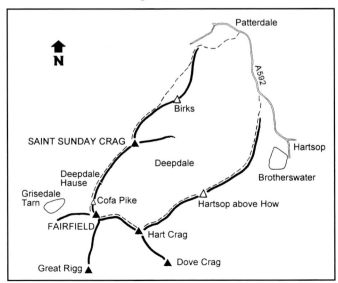

Looking back to Greenhow End on Fairfield, from Hartsop above How

HIGH STREET 2717ft/828m

Lakeland's highest fell east of the Kirkstone Pass, High Street is a fine mountain with a wealth of interest. For those with a sense of history, High Street offers a Roman road (hence the name) and was also the location of horse races, recalled in today's little known alternative name, Racecourse Hill. The greater fame stems from its adoption by those indomitable Romans for the creation of their 'highway in the sky', linking forts at Ambleside and Brougham. Not for them the relative ease of a route over Kirkstone: if the more direct course involves a climb of well over an additional thousand feet, then so be it.

The Roman road's highest point falls just short of the 2700ft contour west of High Street's summit, and maintains a 2000ft-plus altitude for some seven miles, illustrating the scale of this mighty ridge forming Lakeland's eastern frontier. High Street displays an intriguing shape, its broad top tapering at the north to the saddle of the Straits of Riggindale, but sending out two uniform shoulders to the south, each crossing ill defined boundaries to the satellite tops of Thornthwaite Crag and Mardale Ill Bell. The western flank falls steeply to the head of Hayeswater, leaving only the east face to represent High Street in the beefcake department.

This eastern flank lives up to all aspirations. An outstanding Lakeland profile is lifted to a higher plane by virtue of a ridge emanating from the summit plateau, and gravitating spectacularly to form a narrow headland at the head of Haweswater. This is Rough Crag, which asserts itself midway into a top in its own right, and provides not only a climb unparalleled east of Kirkstone, but also unrivalled views of the cliffs on this intimidating face of the mountain. The scene is completed by the sombre waters of the circular pool of Blea Water at the very foot of the crags.

Approaches to High Street are as rich and varied as its history, with the Rough Crag ridge by far the finest. Next in the pecking order is another Mardale approach, employing the Nan Bield Pass to gain height, from where Mardale Ill Bell is traversed on the gentle upper section of the climb. Most direct course from the south is that of the Roman road, which can be traced from the pastures of Troutbeck. Skirting the flanks of Froswick by Scot Rake, it proves a surprisingly easy climb that deftly outflanks other tops.

Possibly the most popular route onto High Street is that starting at Patterdale, all but the final half-mile being utilised by the Coast to Coast Walk. Although the mountain is anything but evident at the outset, the upland walk by way of Boredale Hause, Angle Tarn and The Knott makes a first class approach as High Street waits patiently on the distant skyline. A round journey can be completed by returning over Thornthwaite Crag, then descending by either Threshthwaite Mouth or Gray Crag.

Armed with the knowledge that horse racing once took place on the summit, arrival on this very flat top should come as no surprise. This is a bleak place, the presence of an Ordnance Survey column having little effect, with a crumbling wall and two sprawling piles of stones adding to the general untidiness. The flat terrain makes this no place for thrilling views, although with no higher ground for some miles it is unquestionably an extensive panorama, from Coniston Old Man to Blencathra.

If not ascending by Rough Crag, then regardless of any intended route of departure, this eastern rim should be sought out. The cairn identifying the start of the Rough Crag descent is a good vantage point for this fine ridge dividing the symmetry of Riggindale from Blea Water's hollow. Haweswater and the heights of Harter Fell and Mardale Ill Bell form a splendid backdrop to this stunning Mardale scene. The possibility of witnessing the magnificent spectacle of England's only nesting Golden Eagles (whose eyrie is close throughout the described walk) is just one further attraction.

ROUTE 12: HIGH STREET

Summits:
Rough Crag   2060ft/628m
High Street   2716ft/828m
Harter Fell   2552ft/778m

Start: Mardale Head (NY 469107). Road-end car park at the head of Haweswater. Seasonal and weekend bus service from Penrith.

Distance: 7 miles/11km   **Ascent:** 2520ft/768m

Maps:
OS 1:50,000 - Landranger 90. 1:25,000 - Outdoor Leisure 5

A broad path leaves the car park to quickly fork at a wall corner. The wallside path descends to cross Mardale Beck flowing into the head of Haweswater, then doubles back with the slender finger of the reservoir. The wooded spur of the Rigg, ahead, cloaks the foot of the object ridge, and as the path rises towards the wall and plantation at its brow, a grassy path turns into the bracken to commence a stirring ascent.

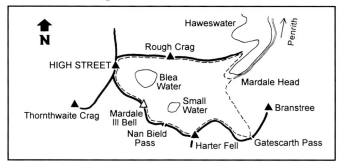

In the company of the old wall the path remains clear throughout, and the surroundings increase in grandeur as height is gained. At an early grassy saddle, a gap in the wall lends itself to an appraisal of the Riggindale scene. The path keeps to the south of the initially craggy crest, but ultimately gains it to enjoy views across Riggindale to the peak of Kidsty Pike. Becoming broader, gentler and grassier, Rough Crag's summit appears in front, backed by the powerful wall of its parent fell. A short, steeper pull could almost be fashioned into a simple scramble before the short walk to the rocky summit.

Ahead is the great wall of High Street, while below are the sombre waters of Blea Water's circular pool. The path descends to a col, Caspel Gate, from where an easy escape route drops left to Blea Water. The ascent resumes less steeply than anticipated, the situation being dramatic without ever being airy, then suddenly the path emerges onto a contrastingly spacious plateau. High Street's summit lies to the south-west, and a wall traversing it from north to south ensures it is soon found.

The walk resumes south on a path following the wall, until branching south-east over tame upland slopes towards Mardale Ill Bell. This minor top is no more than a temporary halt in High Street's decline to the Nan Bield Pass, yet only a few yards north of its cairn one can glean a classic bird's-eye view of Blea Water backed by High Street. On steepening ground the path graduates to the Nan Bield, a major walkers' crossroads. This finest of all Lakeland's mountain passes is occupied by the unique feature of a shelter. For a quicker but still excellent conclusion a good path descends north to the impressive mountain tarn of Small Water, before continuing down the track to Mardale Head.

From the neat defile of the Nan Bield Pass the ridge-walk continues over the upper contours of Harter Fell, the arm extending down to the pass offering an enjoyable pull above impressive northerly views down to Haweswater. The climb ends abruptly with a grassy stroll over a plateau to a wrought iron embellished summit cairn. The bizarre cairn is insufficient recompense for the dull top, the grassy plateau denying any intimate views from Lakeland's easternmost 2500-footer. Features to the south include the slender cone of Ill Bell, and more distantly Morecambe Bay and the peak of Ingleborough in the Yorkshire Dales.

Descent with a fence over the grassy north-east shoulder leads to a magnificently sited cairn overlooking Haweswater. The ridge twists here to drop to the crest of the Gatescarth Pass. Turning north this old track makes an infallible return to the roadhead.

Walkers on the High Street Roman road north of the summit, looking to The Knott, Twopenny Crag and Rampsgill Head

RED SCREES 2546ft/776m
CAUDALE MOOR 2503ft/763m

Red Screes is a whaleback mountain, staunchly independent yet offering reasonable links with Caudale Moor to the east and Dove Crag to the west. The layout is simple, a broad girth with tapering ridges falling sharply to the north and gradually south, to Ambleside. The east flank falls to the Kirkstone Pass, enclosing two impressive combs directly beneath the summit plateau, which is decorated by a sizeable tarn. The summit overlooks the Kirkstone road, where model cars make laborious uphill progress: glancing across at St. Raven's Edge on Caudale Moor, however, there is no indication of the deep trough of Kirkstone in between. The hill's relative isolation guarantees first-rate views, with ranges and groups to east and west, and distant lake scenery to north and south.

Numerous lines of ascent provide something to suit every taste. At almost 1500ft/457m the Kirkstone Pass is Lakeland's most elevated road, and atop it stands the Kirkstone Pass Inn, one of the highest half-dozen pubs in the country. Conveniently sandwiched between both this chapter's fells, it is dominated by the brooding wall of Red Screes, a thousand feet of untamed fellside which are no deterrent to those seeking the most expedient route to any high mountain in the Lake District. Though inevitably steep, the ascent is less tortuous than first appears: the rivers of stone that give the mountain its name are much in evidence, but these unstable runs are easily escaped during the climb.

Less demanding routes exist from Ambleside and Patterdale, by way of either the Scandale Pass, reached from Hartsop Hall by way of Caiston Glen, or from Ambleside by the long green floor of Scandale. Also available are the ridges extending north and south:

that to the north pulls no punches, making a sustained assault on Middle Dodd before easing out to skirt the north-east comb and thus gain the summit.

Contrast this with the long south ridge, accessed by a green lane off the Kirkstone road (the 'Struggle') a mile out of Ambleside. This paces itself for a less eventful ascent, possibly unique in that it extends for several astonishingly easy miles: with no intervening tops to break up the climb, one is apt to forget the object of the outing, but it remains an admirable exercise for the legs on an excellent path.

Caudale Moor is a mountain of immense girth, and although it is more prominently named Stony Cove Pike on modern maps, wanderers across its top will deem 'moor' far more appropriate than 'pike'. The mountain has extremely well defined natural boundaries. To east and west are Threshthwaite Mouth and the Kirkstone Pass respectively, while to north and south it despatches ridges which descend to valley level as far apart as the shores of Brotherswater and Windermere. The felltop is a grassy plateau, at the western edge of which is a cairn monument to a former host of the Kirkstone Pass Inn, in view almost a thousand feet below.

Considering the altitude already attained, the ascent of Caudale Moor from the pub is surprisingly prolonged, best feature being the ridge of St. Raven's Edge after an initially steep pull. The most direct climb from valley level commences at Caudale Bridge, just south of the Brotherswater Inn. From here a grooved quarryman's path scales the crisply defined north-west ridge, to emerge on the west side of the summit plateau. The main north ridge of the mountain, meanwhile, descends to Hartsop, from where a climb of two distinct halves can be made. First section is an excellent pull up the ridge-end onto the subsidiary top of Hartsop Dodd, from where the walk changes entirely, into a long, high-level ramble.

The walker's pass of Threshthwaite Mouth, immediately above Threshthwaite Cove, is the key to valley approaches from Troutbeck and Hartsop. The latter path sees more use, and makes a good return route after ascent by the north ridge. The Troutbeck possibilities should not be ruled out however, for a charming if long walk follows the main beck as far as the tributary of Sad Gill, which is then accompanied up to the formation of the short-lived south ridge: a wall guides this unfrequented route to the summit.

ROUTE 13: RED SCREES & CAUDALE MOOR

Summits:
Caudale Moor   2503ft/763m
Red Screes   2546ft/776m

Start: Caudale Bridge (NY 401111). Signposted parking area on both sides of the A592 half a mile south of the Brotherswater Inn, near the foot of Kirkstone Pass. Served by seasonal Bowness-Glenridding buses.

Distance: 7½ miles/12km   **Ascent:** 3133ft/955m

Maps:
OS 1:50,000 - Landranger 90. 1:25,000 - Outdoor Leisure 5 & 7

Caudale Bridge is two minutes north of the car park, from where Dove Crag has already taken on a brilliant stance at the head of Dovedale. A stile/gate by the bridge send a path climbing with the wall above Caudale Beck. At once Brotherswater appears, quickly joined by the eponymous pub. As the wall turns off, the path zigzags up in sunken fashion before slanting across the fellside. At a fork the main branch leaves the direct line by swinging left up onto the ridge proper. By now the head of Ullswater has appeared beyond Brotherswater. The sunken path scales the ridge, angling left of its crest above the side valley of Caudale.

This grand way rises to its goal of Caudale Quarry. Above the old slate workings a fainter path slants back to regain the ridge, a cracking moment as Dovedale re-appears, with Dove Crag, Hart Crag and Fairfield leading round to Saint Sunday Crag. Across the cleft of the pass, Red Screes looks increasingly impressive, with the pub visible on the summit of the pass. At once the going eases a little, and an inviting grassy path strikes up the relatively narrow spur of Rough Edge to ease out at a prominent cairn. Extending views west have brought in Crinkle Crags, Bowfell and the Scafells.

The way runs increasingly faintly around the rim of Caudale Head to a beckoning cairn. From it a similarly large cairn appears across the gentle slope behind, now very much on Caudale Moor's plateau. A thin path aims south-east towards an old wall, to follow a good path (the return route) east; but better to simply strike east past a cluster of pools. Both options lead to an old wall running north-south over the summit, with the cairn 60 yards beyond it.

Returning west with the wall from the junction a short 100 yards south-west of the cairn, a good path follows it unfailingly, with the individual upthrust of Great Gable unmistakeable amid the big mountain line-up ahead. As the way swings down to the left to reveal the 'model' pub far below, a thin trod runs out to the distinctive cairn of the Atkinson Monument, a memorial to two generations of hosts of the pub. The path descends uneventfully to a saddle in front of St. Raven's Edge, most steps crossing the wall to scale this underling on its east side.

On the crest it is a level walk to a massive cairn, by which stage Red Screes is entirely dominant across the pass. Craggy slopes fall away beneath the cairn, so the path runs a little further south to descend a stony gully before crossing then descending with the wall. The path winds down to a stile in the now solid wall, crossing a final enclosure to the road by the Kirkstone Pass Inn.

Left: Looking north to Brotherswater from Caudale Head

From the car park across the road, a path sets forth to face Red Screes. It runs left over level ground before winding up through rocks to the first craggy outcrops. A split offers a gentler left branch or a stony shoot to the right, the latter involving a minor scramble before re-uniting on the grass above. Looking back, the long High Street skyline and the more shapely Ill Bell ridge enter the scene.

Encountering a longer scree shoot, a gentler, spiralling path climbs above its left side to alight onto a good path slanting up from the left, and from this crossroads the easier way is straight up, trending left to work between low outcrops. If turning right on the slanting path, this crosses the head of a scree gully and directly into another, which involves a rough clamber up partly loose rocks. The slopes relent to offer escape out to the right and up onto the grassy top. The easier path emerges just to the left, and the Ordnance Survey column and cairn are just a stroll above, perched airily atop a dramatic northwards plunge to the Kirkstone Pass.

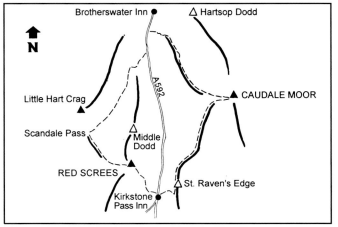

Red Screes from St. Raven's Edge on Caudale Moor

Heading west to commence the descent, the objective is the summit of Scandale Pass. There is little evidence of a path until joining a descending wall, which ushers a path unfailingly down to the crest of the pass, marked by a stile in the wall. The second half of the descent turns right on a path working gently down the upper reaches of Caiston Glen. Caiston Beck soon adds a lively sparkle to this rapid return to the valley, as the path runs down to join a wall and on to approach a small sheepfold at some gates. Through here the path is quickly left by dropping to a stile and footbridge on Caiston Beck in the wall below. Just along the adjacent wall, another stile accesses a footbridge on Kirkstone Beck. Waymarks send the faint path downstream, before swinging around the pasture to a stile back onto the road just short of the start.

THE CHEVIOT 2674ft/815m

The Cheviot is the highest mountain in the range of Border hills to which it gives its name, and the highest ground in England north of Cross Fell. Interestingly, two loftier Scottish hills, Merrick in Galloway and White Coomb in the Moffat Hills, are located further south than Cheviot. The Cheviot Hills are admired more for their haunting loneliness than any dramatic qualities, though some splendid individual landmarks are worth seeking out. The area is characterised by long, slender valleys penetrating deep into the hills, usually occupied by no more than an isolated farm.

Of the Cheviots' six 2000ft hills all but one are exclusively English, and only the Cheviot goes on to attain 2500ft. While it manages this with room to spare, neighbouring Hedgehope Hill boasts a number of finer features. Comb Fell is a morass, while Bloodybush Edge, Cushat Law and Windy Gyle barely scrape the 2000ft mark: the latter has one foot planted firmly in Scotland. Just a mile from the Border fence, Cheviot is characterised by heathery slopes supporting an extensive peaty plateau. All is not dismal however, for the ravines of Hen Hole and the lesser known Bizzle Crags are carved in its northern and western slopes. The minor top of Auchope Cairn overlooks Hen Hole, and its stone men landmarks make this an outstanding vantage point.

The Cheviot has a surly reputation as the final obstacle to Pennine Wayfarers, and this illogical 'out and back' detour should have long since been disentangled from the poor hill. Just reasons are plentiful: on a thirty-mile final section, the last thing anybody needs is a detour; finer Pennine summits than this are sensibly omitted; and though its quagmire reputation has been masked by a 'yellow brick road' of flagstones, without the retracing of PW steps the damage would not have arisen in the first place.

Ascents emanate from the Harthope, College and Bowmont valleys. The former has a long-standing network of permissive paths based on Langleeford, though these are not identified on current OS maps. The finest route gains the long north-eastern ridge of the mountain in the company of the Hawsen Burn. A fence makes a permanent guide to the path over Scald Hill before a steeper pull onto the summit plateau. A more direct route from nearer the farm gains the ridge after a direct slant up a spur of Scald Hill. Less used is a continuation up the valley to just short of Langleeford Hope, where a permissive way climbs to the saddle south-west of Scald Hill. Yet another option is the right of way shadowing Harthope Burn to the the valley head for a steep, easy climb onto Cairn Hill.

The Bowmont Valley to the west is reached from Town Yetholm, thus offering a Scottish ascent route to the Border Ridge. From the farmstead of Cocklawfoot an old drovers' route, Clennel Street, winds easily up by ancient earthworks to the Border Gate, a mile north-east of Windy Gyle. A high-level walk then traces the Pennine Way north-east over King's Seat and up onto Cairn Hill.

The private road along the College Valley is reached from Westnewton to the north, though motor access is by permit only. Two main options leave the valley head, easiest being a path that slants up to the ridge at Red Cribs near a refuge between the Schil and Auchope Cairn, then by the Pennine Way up to the latter's stony scarp. Duckboards lead to Cairn Hill's West top, where flagstones cross onto Cairn Hill for the steady rise to the summit. Sourhope in the Bowmont Valley is an alternative start point for this approach, and indeed for the following one, returning along the Border Ridge. Instead of climbing to Red Cribs, a path follows the College Burn into the ravine of Hen Hole. Beyond some easy clambering past waterfalls, the burn leads up to the plateau near Auchope Cairn. An optional steep climb north out of Hen Hole to a tall beacon on a rash of boulders precedes a curve south around the plateau edge towards Cairn Hill.

Hedgehope Hill from Long Crags

ROUTE 14: THE CHEVIOT

Summits:
Hedgehope Hill   2342ft/714m
Comb Fell   2139ft/652m
The Cheviot   2674ft/815m

Start: Harthope Valley (NT 953225). Roadside parking before a bridge on the inflowing Hawsen Burn, half a mile short of Langleeford. A sign 'limit of access land, no parking beyond this point' confirms the place.

Distance: 10 miles/16km   **Ascent:** 2887ft/880m

Maps:
OS 1:50,000 - Landranger 80 and either 74 or 75
1:25,000 - Outdoor Leisure 16

Leaving Hedgehope Hill on the horseshoe to the waiting Cheviot

From the outset the ascent onto Hedgehope Hill can be fully appraised, fronted by the inviting landmark of Housey Crags. A path shadows Hawsen Burn down to a footbridge on Harthope Burn, then climbs out of the trees and up a field-side. On the open fell the path rises to the rear of Housey Crags, and amid some scrambling options, time can be taken to survey the walk around the dalehead to the Cheviot. Marked by stakes the path makes the short crossing to Long Crags, where a miniature rock ridge forms.

Running along its crest brings a premature end to the day's rock architecture, and the cone of Hedgehope now beckons. From a fence-stile below, a path crosses a broad saddle to the foot of the steep upper flank. The path undertakes a straightforward climb, fading a little as it converges with a fence above the upper limits of a plantation on the south side. The unmistakeable summit features a huge cairn, now a multi-purpose shelter incorporating an Ordnance Survey column. Only on arrival here do the great rolling waves of the Cheviot Hills present themselves westwards.

The next summit, Comb Fell, appears less appealing, for its plateau top is a far cry from Hedgehope's firm footing. The continuation simply traces the same fence all the way, encountering marshy ground on Hedgehope's western shoulder before a pleasant drop to the col. Concerted wet terrain leads onto a felltop whose highest point is open to question, though it is allegedly at this near end of the long, pool-bedecked plateau. The way resumes westward with the fence, dropping to a junction. Though a clearer path goes off south to the prominent alp of Coldlaw Cairn, the watershed route takes the right branch, a much fainter path vaguely keeping to the fence's dog-legs down to the saddle at the head of the Harthope Valley.

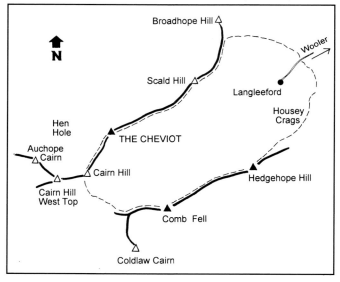

The slopes of the Cheviot's shoulder, Cairn Hill await, and the fence takes the obvious line. Largely free of boggy ground, a steep section relents to reach a fence junction on the top of Cairn Hill (2549ft/777m), marked by a wind shelter (Scotsman's Cairn) from where the last stage to the Cheviot can be surveyed. The fence guides the Pennine Way detour north-east onto Cheviot's summit, the arrival of a winding trail of flagstones making light of what was previously a nightmarish wallow. The flags are drawn in to the unworldly sight of the Ordnance Survey column, its base exposed for several feet out of a moat of black peat.

Unfortunately for the resumption east with the fence, the flags quickly disappear and near-level peaty ground is faced. The peat grounds end where rashes of stones have been transformed into numerous cairns atop the start of a steeper drop of the east ridge. This is a rewarding moment, with the unfrequented, colourful country of the northernmost Cheviot foothills rolling away to the north. The main path crosses to the south side of the fence, though a thinner trod remains on the north. An intervening level spell takes in the minor top of Scald Hill (1801ft/549m) before the descent resumes, and at an angle in the fence a direct path breaks off for Langleeford.

Staying with the fence, a drop to a heathery defile precedes a tiny re-ascent and level section to a gate just under Broadhope Hill. A transverse path turns east to finally abandon the ridge, and as the beginnings of Hawsen Burn appear in front, it curves down towards a line of shooting butts. However, the true path strikes a direct course down towards the stream, becoming clearer in bracken to run parallel with the burn in its attractive ravine. This grand finish traverses the heathery flank, passing an old circular sheepfold and being joined by a bridleway from the left. At a fork the broader way drops down to cross the stream, but the original path maintains its course well above it to shortly drop down to the road bridge.

CROSS FELL 2930ft/893m

The Cross Fell massif is the loftiest part of a mighty and largely unfrequented mountain range that stretches 30 miles from Stainmore to the Tyne Gap. Cross Fell is the highest mountain in England outside of the Lake District, and its two neighbours the Dun Fells help form the Pennines' 800-metre trio. Legend attributes its name to the raising of a saint's cross, thus banishing the 'fiends' of its previous title; though only, it would seem, as far as the fell a little further north which now bears that name.

The hill sees as much usage from Pennine Wayfarers as day walkers, and it offers the highest obstacle on their march. The summit is an extensive plateau crowned by a cross-wall shelter, Ordnance Survey column and cairn. Other than its panoramic views, its best feature is the great skirt of angular blocks fringing this irregular top, and decorated by numerous cairns: the western scarp is perhaps the best place to be, a foreground looking out over the lush pastures of Eden to the Lakeland Fells.

The famous north-eastern rivers Tyne (South) and Tees spring to life on the sprawling eastern slopes of the fell, quickly carving deep valleys typical of the North Pennines; while the western flanks, in the manner of the long miles of this chain, fall sharply to the Eden Valley. Of its adjacent high tops, Great Dun Fell is a tortured summit featuring a golf ball and masts overlooking some bizarre mushrooms, the instruments of an air traffic radar station.

A phenomenon unique to the area is the notorious Helm Wind, which can materialise at any point along the western slopes of the North Pennines. This particularly vicious occurrence is most likely to be experienced in Spring or Autumn. On such occasions the long, thin Helm Cloud forms above the fells, while perhaps three miles to the west the Helm Bar is formed of a similar but

Wildboar Scar, Cross Fell, looking across the Eden Valley to Lakeland

dark parallel cloud. The former crashes down the fellside, but will instantly fade when it reaches the Bar. Serious structural damage can be left in its wake, and it may last for days on end. Many have experienced strong winds on Cross Fell and incorrectly attributed them to the Helm, but there should be no mistaking when the real Helm is 'on'.

The knowledge that the Pennine Way traverses the felltop immediately suggests two obvious lines of ascent. The traditional northward route gains the heights from Dufton, coming first over Knock Fell and therefore making this a lengthy hike: from this direction, an easier way is to start from Knock, following another path up onto the service road - which of course offers itself for an unnatural route from the outset. The PW descent route to Garrigill, in the South Tyne Valley, is another lengthy ascent line, though

very well graded with a long spell on an old fell lane. From Dorthgill, higher up the same valley, a bridleway follows the Moor House Nature Reserve access road before tracing Trout Beck up onto Great Dun Fell.

Easiest route onto Cross Fell is from Kirkland in the Eden Valley, climbing an old mine track-cum-corpse road to gain the ridge north of the summit, where it merges with the Garrigill route. From Blencarn another bridleway traces an appealing droving way onto the fell, rising with Littledale Beck and around the flank of Grumply Hill to climb through Wildboar Scar. Across rashes of stones a distinct edge is gained at 600m, from where a steady cairned rise towards Tees Head ultimately fades, giving the option of making directly for the plateau edge above.

Yet another bridleway climbs from Milburn, further south again, this time onto Great Dun Fell: this is an unfrequented route up to the Silverband mine, where the official line swings round to join the radar station road. A route from the A686 Hartside road to the north has a start point of 1886ft/575m, and offers a high-level march over Fiend's Fell and Melmerby Fell on largely good terrain.

ROUTE 15: CROSS FELL

Summits:
Cross Fell   2930ft/893m
Little Dun Fell   2762ft/842m
Great Dun Fell   2782ft/848m

Start: *Milburn (NY 655293). Ample parking alongside the green.*

Distance: *14 miles/22½km*   **Ascent:** *2775ft/846m*

Maps:
OS 1:50,000 - Landranger 91
1:25,000 - Pathfinder 578, Outdoor Leisure 31

Facing the school at the top end of the green a road branches left, becoming a rough lane to leave the houses behind. At an early fork the main branch goes up to the right, but an enclosed track runs straight on. The right branch at a junction then precedes further sharp bends, and the last one before the lane expires has a gate pointing the route diagonally across a field centre. The unmarked footpath forges a near straight line through several stiles, dropping down at the end to a wall-stile admitting to the rough pasture of High Slack.

Throughout this walk to Kirkland eyes are trained on the sprawling slopes above, with the Cross Fell skyline largely hidden behind its great scarred flanks. However, even from this modest altitude the Lakeland skyline is distinctive on a clear day, with the High Street, Helvellyn and Blencathra groups all well arrayed.

An intermittent grassy way bears left across the colourful pasture, and the wooded bank of Crowdundle Beck is joined at the upper limit of its trees. Across the beck (difficult in spate) a gate admits into a field, across which the Blencarn drove road is joined alongside the house at Wythwaite. This bridleway runs through a colourful strip of country to gain the open fell just above, and makes a tempting alternative ascent route. A gate gives access to Wythwaite's drive, which is followed out to Ranbeck Farm. On the left before it a field boasts the intriguingly named Hanging Walls of Mark Anthony, early farmers' cultivation terraces. Going left of the buildings the farm road runs out into tiny Kirkland.

Turning right, the lane rising to Kirkland Hall becomes a farm track, and across a couple of pastures the fell proper is gained. This splendid old mine track traverses below the scar of High Cap, high above unfrequented Ardale. On breasting level ground the massive summit table is revealed, and when the track goes left the ascent path runs straight on, cairned at regular intervals. A large shelter is passed on a brow, then virtually flat walking leads to the watershed.

With the skirt of boulders waiting up to the right, branching off at any point will gain the summit plateau, while continuing over the watershed and down a short way will find the Pennine Way descending to a cluster of beacons and shelters overlooking the South Tyne Valley. Visible a short distance further is the bothy of Greg's Hut. The final climb rises east of the boulders and across the plateau to the summit shelter. Only on gaining it does the golf ball on Great Dun Fell appear, though far more appealing is the gloriously wild country to the east. The other North Pennine giant of Mickle Fell exhibits its own massive top some miles to the south.

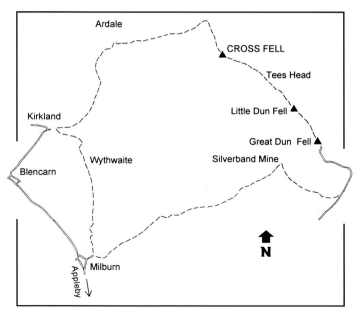

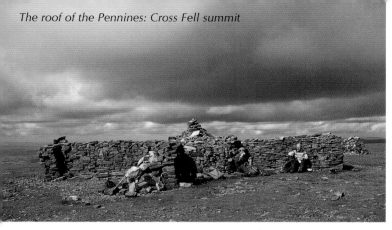

The Pennine Way departs south-east to a sturdy cairn, which in turn points the way to an 8ft tall pillar above the escarpment. The path descends to the saddle of Tees Head (or Crowdundle Head, depending on which scale of map is used), passing a series of high altitude springs and becoming flagged. This peaty watershed is the birthplace of the mighty Tees, and a notice announces entry to Moor House National Nature Reserve. The path escapes the peat and slants up onto Little Dun Fell, which unlike those it sits between is a very uncomplicated top.

Above the pull a good shelter is the product of a rash of stones, as short-cropped grass carpets the brief walk to a simple cairn. Momentarily, Great Dun Fell's golf ball and its attendant paraphernalia appear to be a five minute stroll over level ground, an odd illusion that is soon dispelled. Over to the left is the wilderness of Upper Teesdale, and far to the right the skyline of Lakeland peaks. Man's hand is in evidence on a grand scale, with Cow Green Reservoir to the left, Great Dun Fell's summit directly ahead, and the barytes workings of Silverband to the right under Great Dun Fell's upper slopes.

A few yards from the cairn a grassy descent begins, and a flagged path runs down to the saddle with big brother. On scaling Great Dun Fell the path is deflected around the radar station's perimeter fence to the access road at the other side, the highest surfaced road in England. This runs all the way to the valley, and can be adopted for the initial stage of the descent. Observant walkers will note that a mile of easy walking could be saved by a direct descent from the summit towards the Silverband mine.

After the Pennine Way strikes south for Knock Fell, the road swings down through a ravine to arrive at a rough branch road to the mine. This runs a level course around Great Dun Fell's upper contours, bizarrely so as the summit toys and Cross Fell return to the scene. Reaching a spoil heap in front of the mine, a cairn to the left points the way down pathless slopes. Descending to the north of a conical spoil dump graced with an old pylon from an aerial ropeway that transported ore down to the valley, several more are seen reposed in a line slanting a little down to the left.

Levelling out to a cairn above a small scarp, a descent through the stones bears slightly right to the next plateau. Down again, the head of a sunken green way is located slanting left, the objective being a gate in front of Burney Hill, where the nature reserve is departed. Advancing straight down an improving rough pasture, never far from a wall to the left, a green track ultimately forms to skirt a marshy tract to a gate in the wall below.

A faint way crosses the brow, with two reservoirs down to the left backed by pine trees. A better green track forms to drop to cross a marshy depression and slant up with a plantation wall. At the end of the trees a stile is found in the corner just above, a good point to look back on the last open view of Cross Fell. A wall leads away through more marshy terrain, and encountering several gates/stiles this straight line continues all the way down towards Milburn. Eventually becoming enclosed it winds down to the top of the village to emerge at the head of the green.

MICKLE FELL   2585ft/788m

Mickle Fell is Yorkshire's highest mountain, though since 1974 bureaucrats would have us believe it stands in Durham. The county's only 2500-footer, it thus outpoints all of the Dales' heights to the south, including the celebrated Three Peaks. Mickle means 'big', a description that barely does justice to this great sprawl of moorland culminating in a mile and a half long summit plateau. To its incredible girth must be added its aloofness and its roughness. Set deep within the North Pennines Area of Outstanding Natural Beauty, like its companion Cross Fell much of its environs are also designated a National Nature Reserve.

Mickle Fell's lonely summit rises between Stainmore Common to the south, the Eden Valley to the west, Teesdale to the east and Cow Green Reservoir to the north. Within its vast entourage are the 2000ft heights of Little Fell, Murton Fell and Bink Moss; the headwaters of the river Lune, a tributary of the Tees; while the distant base of the hill is lapped by the parent river itself, which features the mighty waterfalls of Cauldron Snout and High Force tumbling over the rocks of the Whin Sill. The extensive Cow Green Reservoir was completed in 1970 to the despair of conservationists and devotees of wild country, while botanists trawled the moors on hands and knees to salvage rare plants before the flood came. It is then, a little frustrating to see much of the area 'closed' to walkers on the grounds they might damage the fragile habitat.

A great scythe of a summit plateau sweeps east from the county boundary to take in the undefinable high point, a massive pile of stones that effectively claims the summit, and ultimately a distant Ordnance Survey column that is considerably lower at 2487ft/758m. A green track runs the entire length of the plateau, which offers the easiest walking on the hill: it passes wreckage of an aircraft in the low col east of the cairn. Although peaty uplands dominate this landscape, limestone breaks out at surprisingly high locations, including near the bowl of King's Pot where rocky ledges fringe the western end of the summit arc. This is also a landscape of cairns and shakeholes, sheepfolds and lead mining.

On a clear day the summit views are phenomenal, indeed it is difficult to find any noteworthy part of Mountain England omitted: to the west is an extensive Lakeland skyline far beyond the Eden Valley, to the south the Howgill Fells lead to the many peaks of the Yorkshire Dales, with Ingleborough and Whernside seen through the Mallerstang gap; immediately to the north, the rolling heights of the North Pennines are dominated by the Cross Fell group and Burnhope Seat, while much further north are the similarly rounded tops of the Cheviot Hills.

Perhaps Mickle Fell is best known for the infamy of access restrictions. There are no public rights of way to the summit, and approval is only given under certain conditions on certain days. While jealously guarded sporting and conservation interests are not uncommon in these parts, the fact that much of the hill stands within the Warcop artillery range puts Mickle Fell on a different footing. Walkers are discouraged from leaving the negligible rights of way, while the military accept no responsibility for accidents due to the presence of unexploded shells. Live firing can take place up to six days a week, with the quiet day normally Monday: there are occasional longer spells to allow tasks such as sheep gathering. Red flags are flown at main access points to indicate that firing is in progress, which can be confirmed in advance with the Range Officer on 017683-41661. This applies to any chosen route, as the summit itself is within the range, albeit some distance from the main centres of activity.

All approaches to Mickle Fell's summit are lengthy and many are frowned upon: the only ones that will not incur someone's wrath are those for which the landowner's agent is able to

67

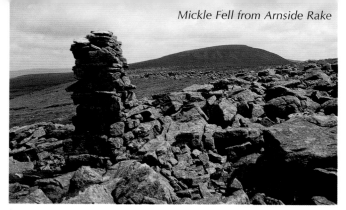
Mickle Fell from Arnside Rake

issue a permit, assuming no conflict with any other activities. On supplying details to Youngs Chartered Surveyors, 3 Wentworth Place, Hexham NE46 1XB a permit may be issued to climb Mickle Fell on a specified date. The only permitted route is the 'Boundary Route', which follows the Strathmore estate/county boundary over the western shoulder of the summit, approached either from the B6276 in the south or Maize Beck to the north: the latter can be reached by several rights of way, but a permit will still be required to ascend to the summit with a clear conscience.

The northern approach from Cow Green (altitude 1640ft/ 500m) follows the Pennine Way through Birkdale farm to reach the mining spoil at Moss Shop. An unmarked bridleway crosses to Maize Beck, which must be forded at Grid Ref. 791263 to follow the fence up to the summit plateau. It should be stressed that Maize Beck is impassable after wet spells: to reach the fence dry-shod would require a detour of the best part of five miles upstream to a footbridge at Maizebeck Scar, then tracing the south bank back - with the same distance to re-tread on the return.

Happily the Maize Beck 'access point' can also be reached by rights of way from the west, and thus the Eden villages of Dufton and Hilton offer the best and the most practicable approaches.

From Hilton, an old mine track traces Hilton Beck beneath the imposing peak of Roman Fell (1949ft/594m) to climb between the steep walls of Scordale, coloured with evidence of an intense lead mining past. Emergence at the valley head into contrastingly open country finds Swarth Beck leading gently down the other side to its confluence with Maize Beck. The untramped bridleway then leads down the south bank to the boundary fence.

From Dufton the landmark of High Cup is the objective, a memorable outing in its own right even if plans to scale Mickle Fell are abandoned. Easiest approach is via the Pennine Way, though a lesser known path from Harbour Flatt, to the south, penetrates the valley floor of High Cup Gill. The remarkable feature is a set of almost uniform converging scars of volcanic Whin Sill rock. At the very head, High Cup Nick, the routes merge in spectacular surroundings. The Pennine Way then crosses High Cup Plain to Maize Beck, and ignoring the PW ford, another untramped bridleway leads downstream to the boundary fence.

The southerly approach from the county boundary on the B6276 Brough-Middleton in Teesdale road gives another elevated start at 1509ft/460m, though this shortest route to the summit can nevertheless prove arduous. The constant presence of a fence makes navigation simple, though the fording of Connypot Beck beneath the brow of Hewitts can be a challenge. At Hanging Seal several parish boundaries meet, and a novel feature of this ascent line is the array of numbered boundary stones by the fence. Only the final pull past King's Pot holds real hillwalking interest.

As a footnote, English Nature has erected several colourful notices on Mickle Fell, headlined: National Nature Reserve - Welcome to Upper Teesdale'. Warnings of 'hidden mineshafts' and 'unexploded ammunition' conveniently serve to deter the hapless walker, who will also be perplexed by the immortal lines 'please keep to the public rights of way'. Quite a challenge, given that there aren't any.

ROUTE 16: MICKLE FELL

Summits:
Mickle Fell   2585ft/788m

Start: *Hilton (NY 735207). There is a small parking area at the head of the tiny cul-de-sac village street. Hilton is 2 miles east of the A66 at Appleby in Westmorland. Appleby station is on the Settle-Carlisle line.*

Distance: *15 miles/24km*   **Ascent:** *2132ft/650m*

Maps: *OS 1:50,000 - Landranger 91. 1:25,000 - Outdoor Leisure 19*

After the last of the red sandstone houses at Town Head the road lose its surface, descending as a rough track through a small common to a gate by Hilton Beck. A barrage of warning notices confirm imminent entry into the military range: assuming no red flag is flying, a level mile's walking traces the beck up to the confluence of Scordale and Swindale Becks. The impressive profile of Roman Fell rears up to the right.

The old mine track fords Swindale Beck and resumes up the main valley, still near-level as steeper scarred and scree-lined flanks close in. The inevitable climbing begins, but after bridging the beck the track soon fades. The former lead workings are most evident here, but as a fainter path takes up the running to rise past a fine waterfall, softer terrain is soon entered. By now the beck is playing hide and seek in its limestone surrounds, and delightful walking leads up this grassy enclave to expire at Scordale Head.

Now firmly on the open fell at virtually 2000ft, the peaty watershed is crossed and a gentle descent north-east begins, with the broad strath of Maize Beck leading the eye to long moorland skylines above Teesdale. A cairn guides a faint path down in the improving company of Swarth Beck, with the objective of Mickle

Fell just across to the right. The broadening beck makes a pleasant companion as it meanders for a good mile down to enter the wide Maize Beck. Its bank leads downstream for a further half-mile to find the county boundary fence coming down to the water's edge.

The bridleway is traded for the access route as boundary stone 101 sets the scene for a steady, fence-side ascent to the Mickle Fell plateau. The rough moorland slopes offer views north to Cow Green Reservoir and the highest Pennines, with the novelty of numbered boundary stones to mark progress. A brief levelling out precedes improved conditions underfoot, with terrain at last more

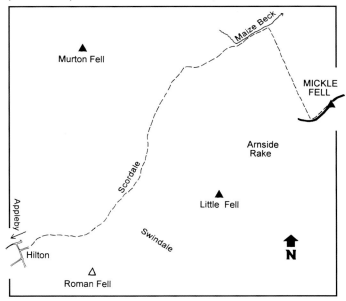

Under King's Pot on Mickle Fell, from one of the many boundary stones on the southern approach

appropriate to a high mountain. Recumbent stone no. 86 announces arrival at the highest point of the fence, on the western shoulder of the summit. While the fence also has a sudden change of direction to circumvent the hollow of King's Pot, it is shunned in favour of a faint, improving path north-east across the plateau. It runs just to the south of the massive pile of stones that act as summit cairn, some 300 yards beyond point 788m.

Departures with the boundary fence are the only routes to comply with permit instructions, either following it south to the B6276 (where a bridleway a little to the west runs back across the Warcop range to Swindale); or back down to Maize Beck, thence either retracing outward steps or following the beck further up to return to the Eden Valley by way of High Cup Nick. The tempting high-level route back across Arnside Rake to Little Fell and thence into Swindale is unofficial.

SCAFELL 3163ft/964m

Though not quite achieving a full 500ft of re-ascent, Scafell's altitude, character and independence ensure it would certainly earn Munro status, rather than being merely a 'top' of Scafell Pike.

Second only to the Pike in England's mountain hierarchy, Scafell is an immense creature that displays its finest wares in one window. From the platform of Mickledore, the narrow connecting ridge with the Pike, the timid walker can gaze with incredulity at the awesome scale of Scafell Crag, Lakeland's finest cliff. From Mickledore it presents an unassailable, almost repelling face; it demands attention yet does its best to deter boarders. A modest cairn crowns the short-lived, stony top, which is always much less populated than the scene to the north-east, where the honeypot platform of the Pike is framed by Scafell Crag's uppermost crags.

Scafell's position makes its ascent only truly practicable from Wasdale and Eskdale. From above Brackenclose at the head of Wastwater, a largely featureless, direct route makes a long haul up the western flank above Rakehead Crags. From Wasdale Head itself, a path by way of Lingmell Gill, Brown Tongue and Hollow Stones leads increasingly roughly up onto Mickledore, where two choices await.

A third, Broad Stand, is most direct, but firmly beyond the capabilities of the non-climbing walker. Faced with the full might of Scafell Crag, the arduous alternatives demand considerable descent from Mickledore before resuming the climb, particularly the sensible option by way of Foxes Tarn on the Eskdale side. This works down beneath the crag to find an inviting gully sending a rough path up to the tarn en route to the summit plateau.

The popularity and consequent erosion of the scramble up Lord's Rake has left it something of a leper, suitable only for those who just can't be told. It runs straight as an arrow beneath Scafell

Crag, initially a deep trench between rock walls set at a trying angle. A long climb to the first col is the toughest section, preferring more solid rock on one side to the shifting stones and choking dust of a dangerously denuded scree shoot: experienced winter mountaineers will find greatest interest here. The full ascent of the Rake is more akin to a roller-coaster, as a less claustrophobic traverse through two further ups and downs brings escape at the end onto a short, rough climb to the felltop.

The Rake's advantage over similar scrambles is its location amidst the rock scenery of Scafell Crag: rarely is the hillwalker afforded such opportunities to enter the preserve of the climber, and his experiences can be transported into the realms of fantasy by branching onto the West Wall Traverse just short of the first col. The enclosing walls of Scafell Crag take on a new dimension as a sloping ledge leads into the yawning chasm of Deep Gill, for an extremely rough clamber through peerless rock architecture onto the summit plateau.

The extensive southern flanks offer a variety of long walks, though approaches from Miterdale and Boot via Burnmoor Tarn are inferior to paths further up Eskdale. Upper Eskdale provides first-class, crowd-free routes over colourful slopes in unsurpassed surroundings. Finest high level approach is the Terrace Route from Wha House, taking in the subsidiary top of Slight Side en route.

The same start also offers a splendid route via Taw House and Scale Bridge to meet the river Esk on Great Moss, while the most beautiful route to the moss follows the river from Brotherilkeld via Lingcove Bridge. The upland amphitheatre of Great Moss is one of Lakeland's greatest settings, above which Cam Spout Crag and its adjacent falls provide company before the path gains the summit by way of tiny Foxes Tarn. The continuation to Mickledore is largely superfluous in view of the temptation of the Foxes Tarn branch, well below the ridge.

Scafell from above Cam Spout

ROUTE 17: SCAFELL

Summits:
Scafell   3163ft/964m

Start: *Eskdale (NY 200009). Start from the valley road above Wha House Farm, a long mile and a half east of Boot, just past the youth hostel. There is a parking area immediately above the road. Dalegarth station at Boot is the terminus of the Ravenglass & Eskdale Railway from Ravenglass, on the Cumbrian Coast railway.*

Distance: *10½ miles/17km*   **Ascent:** *3035ft/925m*

Maps:
OS 1:50,000 - Landranger 89 or 90. 1:25,000 - Outdoor Leisure 6

Two minutes up-dale of the parking area a drive bears off to Taw House, with these early steps dominated by the splendid Harter Fell across the valley. At the farm a permissive path avoids the yards and fields, instead running above the wall on the base of the fell. Early prospects of Bowfell are gleaned as this splendid green path runs on to cross Scale Beck on a stone arched bridge, a good vantage point for the falls immediately upstream.

When the path forks a hundred yards further, the left branch slants beneath Heron Crag. This splendid old way enjoys stylish zigzags up the fellside, and at the top resumes a northward march. Within minutes a corner is turned to reveal an awesome prospect as Esk Pike, Bowfell and Crinkle Crags are joined by the quite stunningly arrayed Slight Side, Scafell Pike and Ill Crag.

The path now runs a near level course, first along the length of a long marsh. Crossing the gentlest of brows the sanctuary of Great Moss is revealed, surrounded by the finest peaks in the land. Also worth picking out are the cliffs of Cam Spout Crag on Scafell's slopes, and Esk Buttress (Dow Crag on maps) on the Pike's slopes.

In between the two is Cam Spout, key to the ascent. The path drops left, curving round to pass through a sheepfold followed by the boulders of Sampson's Stones beneath Cam Spout Crag.

Beneath bouldery slopes the path arrives at Cam Spout, where the rambling ends and the climbing begins. Across the stream the first stage is an extended, simple scramble, which the main path seeks to avoid on the right. Tilted slabs alongside the waterfalls make light work of uphill progress, and on easing out Scafell reveals its true self, as does Mickledore linking it with the magnificent Scafell Pike. The path rises through a confluence and up the tongue into an atmospheric bowl.

Approaching the base of the crags a less obvious grassier path breaks off left from the main path bound for Mickledore. At the foot of the crag it turns left up a well defined gully, clambering up boulders which make for rapid and absorbing progress: this dead straight line between rock walls offers optional scrambling. On emerging it maintains the same line to arrive at the hollow of Foxes Tarn, a tiny pool half-filled by a large boulder.

The final section is surprisingly easy, a built path zigzagging up otherwise tortuous scree slopes onto Scafell's summit plateau. While the cairn stands just to the south, in good conditions a right turn will find the head of Deep Gill two minutes away, from where the sheer walls of Scafell's crags are displayed in no uncertain terms. Across the gully rises the majestic Pinnacle, while the spectacularly sited top of Symond's Knott hovers to the left above Deep Gill Buttress. A rocky clamber leads to its cairn, a delectable perch from which to gaze down over the cragtops into the fearful abyss. While Wastwater and the Pillar group are suddenly revealed in style, it is the immediate rock architecture that will stay in the memory.

Having devoured the grandeur, the saddle to the south sees several paths unite for the brief pull to Scafell's summit cairn. From this stony top Symond's Knott appears of equal height and far more deserving of summit status. Across the undetectable void of Mickledore the solid looking top of the Pike asserts superiority to a far greater extent than the mere fifty or so feet that separate this celebrated pair. As a viewpoint Scafell is extensive rather than exciting: Burnmoor Tarn shimmers on one side, above Wastwater, while on the other side are the upper recesses of Eskdale.

The return heads south along the ridge, soon revealing Slight Side below, and then the nearer Cam Spout Crag. A largely clear path keeps to the highest ground, falling to a grassy saddle where the faintest of rises leads to the cairn atop Cam Spout Crag. This is an outstanding platform for surveying the Scafells, including in the foreground the route from Cam Spout. Resuming, a briefly stony slope precedes a short, easy walk along to Slight Side. Least visited of the Scafell group tops, this marks a sudden termination of Scafell's south ridge, and the end of this walk's drama.

The summit consists of twin rock bosses split by a narrow defile, the highest being the cairned western one. The view stresses Slight Side's affinity with Eskdale, for the entire valley is gazed upon, the course of this most beautiful river being traced from the wilderness of its beginnings beneath the highest mountains, through the colourful mid-valley country below Harter Fell and Hard Knott, to its lazy miles preceding entry into the sea at Ravenglass.

The path passes through the gap and slants left to avoid craggy ground. Ignoring an early, eroded branch right, a slimmer way continues down before swinging back right down onto grassy slopes. This marks the end of any roughness, and a thin, clear path resumes down gentle grass, intermittently cairned and angling slightly left. Approaching the marshy Cowcove basin the path turns right to traverse high above it to the smaller, higher level Catcove basin. Though occasionally faint the presence of cairns dispels any doubts as to the path's course.

As the stream drops through a ravine at the end of the marsh, the path forges straight on its near-imperceptible descent.

Another marshy basin is crossed at the outset, and at the end the outflowing trickle is crossed to resume as before. Not for nothing is this splendid path known as the Terrace Route, as it angles down to more fully reveal the Brotherilkeld environs. After joining a wall below to drop to a corner-cum-sheepfold, the parking area is quickly revealed below, a bull's-eye finish.

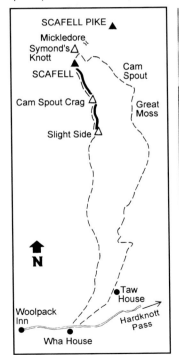

Slight Side fronting Scafell, seen from Catcove Beck

Unlike England, Wales is a predominantly hilly country, and the mountains of Snowdonia provide the vast majority of its high peaks. However it is perhaps only the Glyders, Cadair Idris and Snowdon itself that have achieved a popularity consistent with Lakeland's many favourites. As in the Lake District, the dominant feature of the main hills is the legacy of the Ice Age, with craggy north and east facing cliffs frowning over dark, scooped cwms, often sheltering small lakes held back by glacial moraines.

Snowdonia's hills fall into what are largely well defined groups: from Conwy Bay to Mid Wales are ranged the Carneddau, the Glyders, Snowdon, Moel Siabod, Moel Hebog and the Nantlle Ridge, the Moelwyns, the Rhinogs, the Arenigs, the Arans, the Berwyns, the Dovey Forest and Cadair Idris. Though not all these groups attain sufficient height to feature in this book, they are all very much integral parts of the Welsh mountain scene. The northernmost groups are very much the big three, and these include all of Wales' 3000-footers.

The rolling hill of Mid Wales rarely manage even to break the 2000ft mark, yet offer some of the most rewarding hillwalking in the land. Ultimately they lead to the Brecon Beacons, a name chosen for the National Park that includes, again, several very well defined groups. Westernmost is Mynydd Ddu (the Black Mountain), also known as the Carmarthen Fan, followed by the little known Fforest Fawr. Next is the eponymous group that is highest and by far the most popular: Pen y Fan fails by less than a hundred feet to earn the Brecon Beacons a 3000-foot peak. Finally the Black Mountains reach over to the English border. While much of this hill country is gentle and rounded, the two most impressive groups plunge away to the north to provide dramatic escarpments of red sandstone.

Major centres for the heart of Snowdonia are Capel Curig, Llanberis and Beddgelert, with Ffestiniog, Bala, Dolgellau and Dinas Mawddwy all making useful bases. In the Brecon Beacons, Brecon itself is most convenient for all the mountain groups, with Crickhowell, Talgarth and Sennybridge also usefully placed.

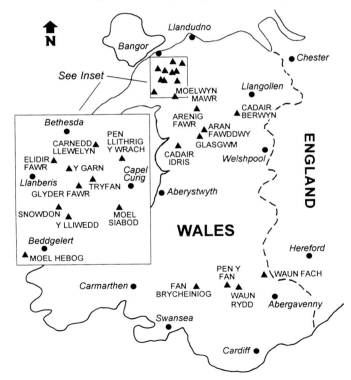

On the flanks of Moel Hebog
Opposite: Snowdon from Y Lliwedd

CARNEDD LLEWELYN 3491ft/1064m
PEN LLITHRIG Y WRACH 2621ft/799m

Carnedd Llewelyn, the second major peak of England and Wales, is the zenith of a vast rolling mountain country reaching from the Ogwen Valley, across which its slopes trade glances with the Glyders, to the coast at Conwy. Collectively known as the Carneddau, this is by far the greatest high level tract south of the Scottish Highlands, barely straying beneath the 3000ft contour for some 5½ elevated miles between Pen yr Ole Wen and Foel-fras.

'Llewelyn's cairn' occupies a broad summit, to the east of which craggy slopes fall to a secretive cwm cradling a tiny pool, Ffynnon Llyffant. This exposed summit can feel a bleak and lonely place when the first tinges of dusk materialise, or when icy winds impart further urgency to the short hours of winter daylight. Navigation can prove particularly difficult in poor conditions, and the safety of the valley can seem, and often is, very distant. Llewelyn was a Welsh prince whose family aspired to rule the country in the late 13th century. After his downfall in battle, he was replaced as Prince of Wales by his younger brother Dafydd, though he too met an untimely and violent demise. In hierarchical fashion, Dafydd is remembered on the second summit of the group.

Three major ridges radiate from Carnedd Llewelyn, two heading towards the heart of Snowdonia, the other rolling north over a number of less dramatic tops towards the Bwlch y Ddeufaen and ultimately the sea. The principal ridge winds down over Carnedd Dafydd to Pen yr Ole Wen, from where exceptionally steep slopes fall to Llyn Ogwen. Carnedd Dafydd's northern face is an awe-inspiring sight, best appraised from Yr Elen in favourable lighting. It is more intimately inspected, however, from the path along the crest of Ysgolion Duon - the Black Ladders - en route to Carnedd Llewelyn. A line of cliffs also extend west from the summit, harbouring a series of small scooped cwms.

The second ridge runs south-east to present a switchback ride over Pen yr Helgi Du and Pen Llithrig y Wrach, impressive 2500ft peaks in their own right. The fact that the latter is the only other Carneddau peak to assert itself by as much as 500ft is, not surprisingly, largely lost on most hillwalkers. Certainly it feels far less bootprints than the summits grouped more closely around Carnedd Llewelyn. Llewelyn's link with Pen yr Helgi Du is forged at the charismatic Bwlch Eryl Farchog, above which are the only sections of main ridge that demand hands out of pockets. On the north-eastern side is Cwm Eigiau, the upper section of which is frowned upon by the famous cliff of Craig yr Ysfa: the slow progress of climbers can often be appraised from the ridge.

The ridge to the north embraces three further 3000ft tops, and though all are plainly subservient to Carnedd Llewelyn, such are their extent and their altitude that they have rightly merited a separate chapter. To complete Carnedd Llewelyn's pivotal role, a short arm extends west to the outlying peak of Yr Elen. Its neat summit encases the superb Cwm Caseg, again holding a tiny pool, before falling to the valley at Bethesda.

Most ascents spring from the Ogwen Valley to the south, where the scenery is finest and the altitude an inviting thousand feet. A direct route onto the tops is a no-holds-barred clamber up Pen yr Ole Wen's south ridge from the road bridge on the outflow of Llyn Ogwen. This relentless 2000ft haul gives memorable views back to the Glyders and Y Garn. A less demanding ascent from the east end of Llyn Ogwen takes a path up to Cwm Lloer, which is occupied by one of the numerous little sheets of water that frequent the Carneddau cwms. From here a grand scramble up the east ridge onto Pen yr Ole Wen's summit is followed by easy high level walking over Carnedd Dafydd to Carnedd Llewelyn.

Pen Llithrig y Wrach from Creigiau Gleision, with Tryfan, Y Garn, Pen yr Ole Wen and Carnedd Dafydd beyond

Approaches from the west embrace Carnedd Dafydd's north-west ridge, a hugely rewarding route from the upper limits of Bethesda which increases in grandeur as a well defined edge forms. The satisfaction of this ascent line invites a sweeping horseshoe by returning from Carnedd Llewelyn over Foel Grach and Drosgl, though a shorter one awaits by descending instead over Yr Elen, whose west ridge also makes a fine way up.

The most direct ascent to Carnedd Llewelyn makes use of a reservoir service road to Ffynnon Llugwy from the A5 west of Helyg, a path continuing onto the ridge at Bwlch Eryl Farchog above Cwm Eigiau, for a climb along the ridge to the summit. This by-passes Pen yr Helgi Du, which itself possesses a good ascent route up its shapely south ridge of Y Braich. This would make a good shorter 'horseshoe' of Afon y Bedol by returning over Pen Llithrig y Wrach.

This latter peak can be ascended from Capel Curig by a bridleway to the bwlch overlooking Llyn Cowlyd Reservoir, then up the broad south ridge. The Cwm Eigiau horseshoe is a popular route from the north-east, and easily combines the two object peaks. Approaches to Carnedd Llewelyn from the north are generally longer and involve traversing intervening tops, the aforementioned 3000ft peaks which are featured in Chapter 32.

ROUTE 18:
CARNEDD LLEWELYN & PEN LLITHRIG Y WRACH

Summits:
Pen yr Ole Wen   3209ft/978m
Carnedd Dafydd   3425ft/1044m
Yr Elen   3156ft/962m
Carnedd Llewelyn   3491ft/1064m
Pen yr Helgi Du   2733ft/833m
Pen Llithrig y Wrach   2621ft/799m

Start: *Llyn Ogwen (SH 668605). Glan Dena stands at the eastern end of the lake. Roadside parking. Served by Snowdon Sherpa buses from Bethesda and Capel Curig.*

Distance: *12½ miles/20km*   **Ascent:** *4468ft/1362m*

Maps:
OS 1:50,000 - Landranger 115. 1:25,000 - Outdoor Leisure 17

The drive past the house at Glan Dena runs on to approach the farm at Tal y Llyn Ogwen. Just before it a path is directed up the wallside to a stile. Advancing a short way to a marker post, further occasional posts point an intermittent path up through a rough pasture, reaching the Afon Lloer after rising by a sidestream. Across, a clearer path rises alongside the west bank amid some colourful falls. Looking back, the pyramid of Tryfan presents a

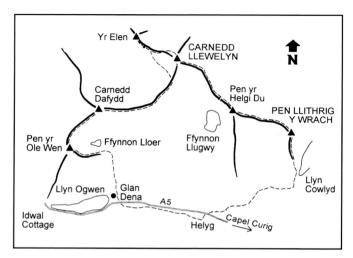

quite improbable aspect. The path climbs through bracken to a wall-stile, and up again to swing left, revealing the east ridge of Pen yr Ole Wen with its summit towering over.

Just short of the mountain lake Ffynnon Lloer, a branch breaks off left to an unpromising craggy bluff at the foot of the ridge. Several straggly paths merge to reach the base of the cliff at some quartzite rocks, where an obvious line involves a simple scramble. Above it a clear path takes a surprisingly easy line through stony outcrops, enjoying fine views down into Cwm Lloer. Only towards the top does the going ease, and the sprawling summit cairn occupies the eastern end of the summit plateau.

The continuing path quickly reforms to the west, curving round the head of Cwm Lloer and losing only a little height at Bwlch yr Ole Wen. The steady climb onto Carnedd Dafydd passes

On Yr Elen, looking east over Cwm Caseg to Foel Grach beyond the slopes of Carnedd Llewelyn

two massive ancient piles of stones-cum-shelters, the latter of which is just short of the main cairn. Carnedd Dafydd is lowest of the select band of four 1000 metre peaks south of the Scottish border.

Carnedd Llewelyn awaits two miles distant, a simple stroll in decent conditions. The path runs east above Ysgolion Duon, a sensational craggy plunge featuring spiky aretes at the top of the Black Ladders. Little height is lost, and at the end the path drops to Bwlch Cyfryw-drum. A brief arete precedes a similarly moderate rise onto Carnedd Llewelyn, the path winding up steeper, stony slopes to the summit. However, very shortly after starting the climb, a detour left brings in the outlying Yr Elen. Contouring round the western flank of Carnedd Llewelyn leads to the bwlch linking with Yr Elen, where a well worn path enjoys a short climb north-west above Cwm Caseg to the summit. Back at the bwlch a longer climb leaves the rim of the cwm to ease out on Carnedd Llewelyn's broad top, crowned by a scrappy shelter and sprawling cairn.

Departing south, an improving path swings left to descend impressively above the craggy eastern face. This winds pleasantly down stony slopes, soon easing out and running along to a rocky little crest. Down to the left are the mighty cliffs of Craig yr Ysfa above Cwm Eigiau, and the path shows solidarity with a sustained steeper drop culminating in a scrambly descent to the Bwlch Eryl Farchog. Crossing this narrow crest to the bwlch, Pen yr Helgi Du thrusts engagingly in front. A gentle grassy rise leads to the base of jagged rocks, though the pull through them is easy and quickly accomplished. Two minutes further the summit plateau is gained, and from the corner cairn a thin path runs south-east on grass to the main cairn, a skilfully built pillar alongside a scrappy cairn.

Resuming south-east, another cairn sees a path quickly re-form to drop down above a craggy northern drop. A prolonged grassy amble descends to the broad Bwlch y Tri Marchog, with the big valley of Cwm Eigiau down to the left. Crossing a fence-stile at the far end, the longer plod up Pen Llithrig y Wrach begins, the path correspondingly fading in tandem with the contours. The summit cairn sits at the eastern end of a plateau, just yards from a steep easterly drop to Llyn Cowlyd Reservoir.

Departing south, a thin path forms above the eastern edge, though it might be lost as it swings away from the edge. If retained it leads delightfully down through heather and other vegetation in the direction of the reservoir head. Devotees of Lakeland will see a resemblance to the Wastwater Screes across the lake. Towards the bottom the bridlepath running just above the water makes an obvious goal. Five minutes' steady rise on this leads to a bridge on the feeder stream: without crossing, a ladder-stile just above is the objective. The stream's relative size is explained by the presence of a major water channel built to drain the southern slopes of these hills in order to supply the reservoir on the north side.

A substantial bridge on the left leads over two branches of the leat, and swinging right to reach a smaller footbridge, a stile accesses the leat-side. A smashing path follows this west for about half a mile, with Tryfan and the Glyders ahead. Passing several bridges the leat prepares to make a big loop to hold its contour, and is left by a bridge when a broad path drops away, bound for farm buildings some distance below. A boggy area is negotiated towards the bottom, to continue downstream to the slab bridge of Pont y Bedol.

From a bridle-gate across the bridge, a ladder-stile can be ignored to remain on the wallside past a house, and on to another ladder-stile in the wall. Beneath the white-walled Tal-y-braich-uchaf a grassy access track slants amiably down to the A5 just past the climbers' hut of Helyg. Across the road a good path runs along to join the old road from Capel Curig to Ogwen, long superseded by Thomas Telford's present highway. Increasingly dominated by Tryfan, it takes a variety of guises as it passes by the farms of Gwern Gof Isaf and Gwern Gof Uchaf to emerge onto the road opposite the start.

The Carneddau from Craig Wen, to the south-east; featuring Pen yr Ole Wen, Carnedd Dafydd, Pen yr Helgi Du, Carnedd Llewelyn and Pen Llithrig y Wrach

GLYDER FAWR 3278ft/999m
TRYFAN 3002ft/915m

Leaving the shattered summit of Glyder Fawr

Sandwiched between the massifs of the Carneddau and Snowdon, the Glyders are second only to the latter in popularity. Indeed many would judge this magnificent range superior to the country's highest peak. Containing no less than five 3000ft mountains, the chain extends in a lazy 'V' around Llyn Ogwen, almost to a man turning their backs on the Pass of Llanberis to the south.

At the very heart of this group is the sanctuary of Cwm Idwal, a beautiful setting for the sizeable Llyn Idwal to repose in. Cwm Idwal is a National Nature Reserve, highly valued for rare arctic-alpine plants that survive amongst the cliffs. The lower ground of the cwm is regularly to be found alive with parties of students, though the site extends far beyond the shores of the lake to take in the craggy skylines and summits hovering above.

A series of deep cwms slotted in between ridges and spurs of varying roughness interrupt the steep northern edge of the range, and above Cwm Idwal can be found the delectable Cwm Bochlwyd. With its own beautiful little lake, this is a masterpiece of glacial endeavour, and sheltering as it does beneath Tryfan, the Bristly Ridge of Glyder Fach, and Y Gribin, surely boasts the finest setting of any such cwm in the country. Frowning less benevolently over Cwm Idwal is the Devil's Kitchen (Twll Du - the 'Black Hole'), a veritable Glyders institution featuring an intimidatingly dark cleft between dripping cliffs. Less well known is the hanging valley of Cwm Cneifion, the Nameless Cwm, which shuns the crowds from its hidden position high above the Idwal Slabs.

This chapter deals with the eastern half of the group, the Glyders proper, featuring both the highest peak in the range, Glyder Fawr, and the most popular one, Tryfan. In between stands Glyder Fach, no shy wallflower itself, indeed for overall quality it actually surpasses its higher sibling.

Glyders Fawr and Fach have little height difference and are linked by easy slopes, but their summits are renowned for an unusual assemblage of splintered rocks. These are to be seen at their most remarkable on Glyder Fach. The true summit is itself a chaotic jumble of such rocks, even requiring a modest clamber to attain. Close by stands the celebrated Cantilever, a massive slab on which many a large group has posed for photographs without ever hinting it might tilt by as much as a millimetre. Also nearby stands Castell y Gwynt, the 'Castle of the Winds', whose bristly character suitably epitomises these peaks. Again outshining its loftier brother, Glyder Fach claims the pinnacled arete of Bristly Ridge, one of the more breathtaking of scramblers' routes.

Rescue helicopter over Cwm Idwal: looking from Tryfan to Y Garn

This leads neatly onto the third of this esteemed trilogy, the fiercely independent Tryfan. This is a mountain recognised early in any apprenticeship of the hills - let's face it, one sighting of this noble pyramid is enough to ensure its permanent place in the memory box. Tryfan rises triumphantly above the eastern end of Llyn Ogwen, and can prove an alarming sight for motorists on the A5 at its foot, let alone a nervous walker embarking on his first ascent. Exceedingly rough, craggy flanks defend the summit, so it may come as a surprise that several hillwalkers' routes are available. Less surprising is that the summit lives up to expectations, for it is crowned by a pair of square, upright boulders known as Adam & Eve, and making the bold leap from one to the other is said to earn the 'Freedom of Tryfan'. It could also earn a journey in a yellow helicopter.

Tryfan is linked to Glyder Fach by the saddle of Bwlch Tryfan, and while any ascent guarantees an excellent day, when linked with the main ridge one is engaged upon the pre-eminent

route of its kind. The classic itinerary is a scramble of Tryfan's north ridge, a precursor to a continuation over Bristly Ridge onto Glyder Fach. Ideally, after a visit to Glyder Fawr, a descent by Y Gribin completes a Cwm Bochlwyd horseshoe, and this is about as good as it gets.

The main ascent routes are all well marked. Climbing above the Milestone Buttress just above Llyn Ogwen, Tryfan's north ridge submits 2000ft or so in little more than half a mile, and features a good deal of scrambling on firm rock. A better choice for the faint-hearted is the parallel Heather Terrace, which from above the farm at Gwern Gof Uchaf traverses the eastern flank of the mountain beneath some impressive buttress and ravine scenery, to ultimately climb to gain the south ridge beneath the summit.

The hugely popular route through Cwm Bochlwyd from Ogwen gains the ridge at Bwlch Tryfan, then ascending the gentler, though still rough south ridge. A less inspired path forges a more direct line for the top from the west, while to the east, a path through heathery Cwm Tryfan climbs to meet the Miner's Track which then traverses round to Bwlch Tryfan.

Bwlch Tryfan is also the key to Glyder Fach, the obvious line of attack being the Bristly Ridge. This is a scramble of not dissimilar characteristics to Tryfan's north ridge, though perhaps more exposed and even more enjoyable. In both cases, high winds or wet rock add greatly to the risks, while in winter conditions they become very serious mountaineering challenges. Those overfaced by Bristly Ridge can opt to toil up the scree slopes to its east, or preferably take the Miner's Track from the bwlch, which traverses elegantly around the head of Cwm Tryfan to gain the main ridge near the lovely pool of Llyn y Caseg-fraith, 'Lake of the Piebald Mare'.

Longer ascents from Helig or even Capel Curig, further east, take in the lesser 2500ft summits of Gallt yr Ogof (2503ft/763m) and Y Foel Goch (2641ft/805m) before reaching this point.

The Glyders from the south: Y Garn and Glyder Fawr backed by Pen yr Ole Wen, as seen from Crib y Ddysgl

ROUTE 19: GLYDER FAWR & TRYFAN

Summits:
Tryfan   3002ft/915m
Glyder Fach   3261ft/994m
Glyder Fawr   3278ft/999m

Start: Llyn Ogwen (SH 656602). Roadside car parks on the A5 midway along Llyn Ogwen. Served by Snowdon Sherpa buses from Bethesda and Capel Curig.

Distance: 5½ miles/9km   **Ascent:** 3150ft/960m

Maps:
OS 1:50,000 - Landranger 115. 1:25,000 - Outdoor Leisure 17

Glyder Fach's eastern slopes then offer just a stony pull onto the summit plateau. The Miner's Track, meanwhile, descends from the ridge to the Pen-y-Gwryd Hotel at the junction of the Llanberis, Capel Curig and Beddgelert roads, and therefore presents a rare southern approach. Also from the south is a path climbing from Pen-y-Pass up the broad southern spur of Glyder Fawr.

Other routes from Ogwen are via Y Gribin or the Devil's Kitchen. The ridge of Y Gribin is part of Glyder Fawr but serves both Glyders equally well. The foot of the ridge proper is most easily gained from the outflow of Llyn Bochlwyd, from where a superb climb leads through occasionally rough terrain. The path through Cwm Idwal is the key to the Devil's Kitchen, and beyond Llyn Idwal it climbs steeply on a restored surface beneath the dark cleft, emerging on the ridge by Llyn y Cwn before the rougher upper slopes of Glyder Fawr. This little pool occupies the saddle between Glyder Fawr and Y Garn, and can also be reached by a path from Gwastadnant at the foot of the Pass of Llanberis.

Although Y Garn is the major summit of the western Glyders, it can also be linked with relative ease to the main group: indeed so can the other principal peak, Elidir Fawr, thus fashioning one magnificent high level walk, surely the grandest of its kind in Wales.

This route includes two recognised scrambles, the north ridge of Tryfan and Bristly Ridge on Glyder Fach. An alternative ascent of Tryfan from Ogwen via Llyn Bochlwyd and Bwlch Tryfan is much less demanding, while alternatives to Bristly Ridge are mentioned in the text.

At the end of a parking area under the very foot of Tryfan near the eastern end of the lake (east of the main signposted car park), a stile and kissing-gate give access onto the hill. A stone built path climbs the wallside to the base of the popular climbing wall of Milestone Buttress. The path rises left, under the crag, and climbs roughly to join the ridge proper on a grassy shelf. A stony path rises left to begin the real scramble, and with it various permutations. Good scrambling leads onto another plateau, and here the more serious upper half awaits.

Directly above is a major barrage of solid rock, and first impressions are a shade overpowering. For the most part the line in common use is easy to follow, and the point of no return is reached at a sustained spell of climbing with excellent holds. A

83

Earning the 'Freedom of Tryfan'

base of a gully, for a steady clamber up this enclosed chimney with little choice as to route finding. This is generally the case with Bristly Ridge, more so than Tryfan, and as a result is less complicated: the holds are quite superb and when feeling confident to look back, Tryfan itself adopts a magnificent pose.

Simpler but sustained scrambling follows, as a tilted slab precedes a pair of pinnacles. At the end is the daunting prospect of Pinnacle Gap, the key to which is a steady down-climb to the left, with first-class holds. Across the gap stands the Pinnacle, but just a couple of steps to the right an obvious route can be climbed, passing left of an island block and on to another steeper pull, which quickly brings the serious stuff to an end.

A more obvious path omits any more scrambling worthy of the name, but occasional spikes can be incorporated before gaining the summit plateau. A cairned path leads to Glyder Fach's top, with an obvious detour to visit the Cantilever. The summit itself requires a modest scramble to gain its highest point.

notable landmark is the attaining of an unmistakeable notch in the ridge, which should be crossed with care; beyond, a large boss of rock at the top offers an easy gully on its right, and above it Tryfan's north top awaits. The summit is just beyond, its unique top crowned by the rock monoliths of Adam & Eve.

Leaving the summit, either a stony path or tumbled rocks descend south to a saddle with a ladder-stile in a short section of wall: in front stands the rocky 'Far South Peak', beyond which the way continues rapidly down to the wall at Bwlch Tryfan. Ahead, the craggy face of Bristly Ridge means decision time. Alternative ways to the broad ridge-top cross the stiles and either clamber up worsening scree slopes beneath Bristly Ridge, or preferably taking the Miner's Track around the head of Cwm Tryfan.

For Bristly Ridge, paths climb with the wall to the base of the crags, where a path bears right beneath an outlying outcrop to reach the base further across. A stony pull leads to the obvious

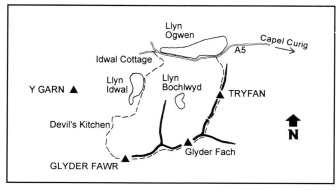

Right: The irrepressible peak of Tryfan, seen from the north-east

Normal walking now takes over on a clear path heading west for Glyder Fawr, though it encounters an early interruption at Castell y Gwynt. While the main path swings around its southern side, survivors of Bristly Ridge will accept a more direct route. On dropping off its far side it will be appreciated this is more of an outcrop than initially appeared. Beyond it the path crosses Bwlch y Ddwy Glyder and forks; the right branch rises to the top of Y Gribin ridge, while the main path slants left for a long steady pull to the top of Glyder Fawr.

Glyder Fawr's summit is set further back than imagined, with numerous bristly tors enhancing this lunar landscape walk, which is particularly inspiring as it rounds the head of the craggy environs of Cwm Cneifion. Glyder Fawr's summit boasts two tors of similar height, the bigger one south-west of that first reached.

A path departs west between the two tops, descending through stones then curving north-west to reach steeper ground. A very rough spiral down through scree reveals the delectable Llyn y Cwn below, and the lower section improves as a wide scree gully leads down to the saddle. The main descent path bears right to merge with another from Llyn y Cwn, and sets off down a curious natural incline. Very soon it reaches a point overlooking Llyn Idwal, and a rebuilt path spirals down to the left into the cauldron of the remarkable Devil's Kitchen. At the base of the ravine a short branch detours left to inspect the outstanding rock scenery at closer quarters. The path continues down to a fork where the left, more direct one is easily missed.

The right branch runs beneath more stunning rock walls then curves down towards Idwal Slabs, encountering a novel stream crossing en route. The path runs beneath the tilted slabs which attract climbers of varying grades, then on the shoreline of Llyn Idwal to its foot. Pen yr Ole Wen dominates straight ahead, while to the right, Tryfan has fully reclaimed its place in the scene. At the outflow the path curves rapidly back down to the start.

Y GARN 3107ft/947m
ELIDIR FAWR 3031ft/924m

With the eastern Glyders covered in the previous episode, there remains much to relish in this western group, and the finest feature is Y Garn. This paragon of a mountain looms high above Cwm Idwal, whose merits are vaunted in the previous chapter. The outstanding profile of Y Garn is equally well appraised from the shore of Llyn Ogwen, its sturdy shoulders seen to support a noble summit. These limbs extend to cradle the delicious hanging valley of Cwm Clyd, in which reposes the tiny Llyn Clyd. Along with its adjacent comrades Y Garn displays the same layout as the eastern Glyders, with an exceptionally steep, craggy and characterful face above Cwm Idwal and the Nant Ffrancon, and tamer slopes falling south-west towards Nant Peris.

The other principal peak is the less brazen Elidir Fawr, which projects as a tapering spur high above Llyn Peris. It is the only one of the nine separate peaks of this ridge to shun the Ogwen Valley, and its indifference is highlighted by suffering at the hand of man. The Llanberis slopes have been quarried away to an alarming scale, though none of this impinges upon ascents from the Ogwen side, nor indeed upon the summit view. More obtrusive to most hillwalkers will be the Marchlyn Mawr Reservoir, whose clinical concrete dam fills an otherwise perfect mountain cwm to the north of the summit.

Across the cwm rises Carnedd y Filiast (2694ft/821m), which harbours its own most impressive cwm to the east, in startling contrast to Marchlyn Mawr. This peak marks the end of the ridge proper, and its northern slopes descend pleasantly out of the National Park boundary to find the base of the hill eaten away by another massive quarry. There is one further mountain to this group, and though not meriting 'Corbett' status, Foel-goch still forms a formidable obstacle sat between the two 'Munros'.

Foel-goch is made to some extent in the fashion of Y Garn. The large numbers attempting the celebrated traverse of the 15 Welsh 3000-footers have forged a well tramped path around its western flank: while this serves a useful purpose, it should not give cause to omit this grand peak from any normal walk. Arrival at the emphatic termination of its summit proves an exhilarating moment, staring down into the deep bowls of Cwm-coch and Cwm Bual, severed by the airy and unassailable ridge of Yr Esgair.

Main ascent routes onto the group are from Ogwen, to the north. The path through Cwm Idwal leads past Llyn Idwal and climbs beneath the Devil's Kitchen to a saddle on the main ridge at the tiny Llyn y Cwn, from where a well worn path ascends Y

Above: Tryfan and Glyder Fach across Cwm Idwal from Y Garn
Opposite: Y Garn from Cwm Clyd

Garn's south-eastern flank. Finest route is a direct assault on Y Garn, via the main north-east ridge from Ogwen: the path winds up to the rim of Cwm Clyd before a super ascending ridge onto the summit.

Foel-goch also has a direct ascent route, though this one is initially less obvious as it works out of Nant Ffrancon towards Cwm Cywion and onto the ridge of Y Llymllwyd. From the south, Nant Peris offers a choice of more leisurely routes, whose great advantages are solitude and the stunning moments of revelation on gaining the main ridge. The main ridge at Llyn y Cwn can also be reached by a path from Gwastadnant at the foot of the Pass of Llanberis. Elidir Fawr can be approached from the Marchlyn Bach Reservoir to the west, ascending the north ridge over Elidir Fach to the steeper upper slopes. This would then point the way to a Marchlyn Mawr 'horseshoe' finishing over Carnedd y Filiast.

ROUTE 20: Y GARN & ELIDIR FAWR

Summits:
Y Garn   3107ft/947m
Elidir Fawr   3031ft/924m
Foel-goch   2726ft/831m

Start: *Idwal Cottage (SH 649603). National Park car park, with extra roadside parking areas on the A5 midway along Llyn Ogwen. Served by Snowdon Sherpa buses from Bethesda and Capel Curig.*

Distance: *7 miles/11km*   **Ascent:** *3215ft/980m*

Maps:
OS 1:50,000 - Landranger 115. 1:25,000 - Outdoor Leisure 17

The main path for Cwm Idwal rises away behind the car park, and within yards another path forks right through a slate cutting. Towards the end the path climbs out to the right, and across to a stile. Ahead is the great Cwm Idwal cradle of hills; Tryfan and the Glyders to the left, Y Garn straight ahead with Foel-goch beyond. The path ambles on along a modest brow, with Llyn Idwal to the left, and Nant Ffrancon down to the right. Another fence-stile interrupts before the intermittent path merges with one from the lake to rise to a prominent gap in a wall. The ascent proper begins as the rebuilt path scales the steep flank, ultimately claiming a hugely satisfying moment as it levels out on the edge of Cwm Clyd, definitely a place to break journey.

The upper section of the ascent scales the inviting arm enclosing Llyn Clyd, and curving south-west it earns fine views to Foel-goch and over the descent route, while Elidir Fawr appears over Bwlch y Cywion. The stiff last stage is partly by-passed by the path which angles left, still steep as it surmounts the summit ridge to gain the cairn. The immediate impact of new views south to the Snowdon group are further reward for this grand moment.

Back at the brow just beneath the summit, a broad path turns north-west down stony slopes to Bwlch y Cywion. Breaking with ridge-walking tradition a broader path forks left to contour the upper slopes of Foel-goch. From the other side of its summit cone this excellent path encircles the head of Cwm Dudodyn, eschewing an obvious line climbing to the minor top of Mynydd Perfedd to work round towards Elidir Fawr.

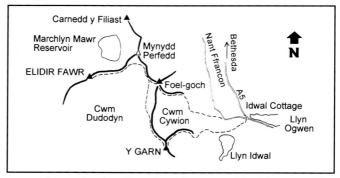

A near level walk to the spiky crest of Bwlch y Marchlyn reveals the deep bowl containing Marchlyn Mawr Reservoir. Though potential scrambles never quite materialise, the path still provides a fine ascent, leading to easier ground and a final stony pull to Elidir Fawr's summit. The main cairn stands just beyond a shelter on this characterful rocky crest extending south-west.

Retracing steps to a stile at the bwlch at the base of Foel-goch's upper contours, a short, steep pull gains the summit, marked by a fence making an abrupt ending in tandem with the flat top. Across the stile the southerly rim of the edge leads dramatically down to a stony col. A path comes in from the right, while up above, Y Garn presents an increasingly sharp aspect. Swinging

A walker ascending Elidir Fawr from Bwlch y Marchlyn, looking north past Foel-goch to Pen yr Ole Wen and the Carneddau peaks

east along the short-lived but colourful crest of Y Llymllwyd, this earns a spectacular view of Foel-goch's craggy face, where feral goats might be seen busily nibbling.

Towards the end of the crest a faint way slants down to the right, tracing an obvious line that meets and shadows an old wall of massive blocks. The trod swings right from this to keep to easier ground, then drops down to the stream of Nant Cywion. Keeping well above a ravine that forms beneath some waterfalls, the stream leads down through an old wall and into bracken to a cross-path. This crosses a simple bridge on the stream but then falters, the key being a ladder-stile seen in a fence down to the left. From it a vague path descends moister ground to meet the old road alongside the climbing hut at Yr Hafod. Idwal Cottage is just a few minutes to the right, beneath the dark shadows of Y Garn.

Snowdon is the biggest of them all, and a superb mountain to claim the crown. Notwithstanding the ignominy of a railway climbing to its summit, to many this is the finest peak in England and Wales. The summit is known as Yr Wyddfa, meaning 'the burial place', though Snowdon's name is now put to use for this entire mountainous area of North Wales. Snowdonia comes from 'Eryri', haunt of the eagle, and though it has been many years since that masterful bird soared high above these cliffs, Yr Wyddfa remains a magnificent vantage point from which to look down on a series of twisting ridges and craggy tops.

The name Snowdon really relates to the entire massif which Yr Wyddfa tops, the very features one looks down upon from the airy summit perch. The view must be shared with train passengers in the tourist season, and in first-class visibility one might see far beyond the Principality to the Lake District, the Isle of Man, the Wicklow Mountains and the Mountains of Mourne. All this and a cafe too, at least when the trains are running.

Ridges radiate in all directions, each encountering at least one separate peak during its course. Yr Wyddfa's less showy side-kick is near neighbour Crib y Ddysgl, also known as Garnedd Ugain. It is more often crossed as a matter of course than ascended in its own right, for it marks the start of Snowdon's finest ridge, heading east to Crib Goch. Narrowly breaking the 3000ft mark, Crib Goch offers a knife-edge arete running a level course above some exceedingly rough flanks. It is sufficiently straightforward to attract large queues in summer, but under winter's mantle it can become a classic mountaineering expedition.

Also branching off Crib y Ddysgl is a contrastingly docile ridge falling north-west to Llanberis, though its eastern scarp throws down a series of craggy walls and unfrequented cwms high above the Pass of Llanberis. It is this approach the railway takes, spreading more than 3000ft of ascent over just 4½ miles. Opened in 1896, its steam and diesel engines runs daily from mid-March to the end of October, subject to the vagaries of the weather.

South-east of Yr Wyddfa, very rough slopes fall to Bwlch y Saethau (Pass of the Arrows), one of the legendary sites of King Arthur's last battle. The ensuing saddle of Bwlch Ciliau meets the prized ridge climbing to Y Lliwedd, a magnificent mountain whose twin peaks just fail to puncture the 3000ft contour. Precipitous crags of clean cut lines plunge northwards towards Llyn Llydaw.

The main arm of the south ridge falls to Bwlch Cwm Llan, across which the ridge resurrects itself to climb to Yr Aran (2451ft/747m), a fine rocky peak that constitutes a satisfying ascent in its own right. One final ridge heading north-west off Crib y Ddysgl features the famous cliffs of Clogwyn du'r Arddu as it falls to Bwlch Cwm Brwynog. Across this pass is a switchback series of rounded tops, Moel Cynghorion (2211ft/674m), Foel Gron (2064ft/629m) and Moel Eilio (2382ft/726m), the least integral of Snowdon's peaks.

Snowdon harbours numerous sheets of water, though the greatest attention seeker is Glaslyn, the 'blue lake' which fills the superb hanging valley in the great bowl beneath Yr Wyddfa and Crib y Ddysgl. The crag-girt face overlooking it saw use as a training ground by the successful Everest expedition of 1953. In the cwm beneath it is the much larger Llyn Llydaw, extended to aid nearby copper mining operations. At valley level more lakes add to Snowdon's string of pearls, the roadside llynnau of Gywnant, Cwellyn and Peris all lapping the massif's broad base.

Y Lliwedd and Llyn Llydaw from Snowdon

90

Not surprisingly Snowdon boasts myriad ascent routes. Certainly the easiest is the bridleway from Llanberis which never strays far from the railway's laboured course. The walk can be enlivened by taking in the northern edges overlooking the Pass of Llanberis. However, even this route can foil the unwary when winter conditions prevail on the convex slopes under Crib y Ddysgl.

From Rhyd-Ddu a path ascends to more interesting ground on Llechog, then climbs above Cwm Clogwyn onto Snowdon's south ridge at Bwlch Main. A variant leaves the Rhyd-Ddu path to continue east onto the start of this ridge at Bwlch Cwm Llan: this is more enjoyably reached from Nantgwynant, by a branch off the Watkin Path at the entrance to Cwm Llan, and passing beneath the peak of Yr Aran. Initially a steep scree climb above the bwlch, the path eases out for a splendid ascent of the entire south ridge.

The full length of the Watkin Path is the better known route from Nantgwynant, a beautiful walk to the old slate quarries in Cwm Llan, above which the path works across the western slopes of Y Lliwedd to Bwlch Ciliau. A steep haul onto the main ridge finds the summit just above. The path recalls the railway magnate who opened it up in 1892, in the company of the then Prime Minister, Gladstone: a massive boulder by the path in Cwm Llan bears a tablet to record the day the 83-year old premier addressed a crowd from it.

The longest approach to Snowdon's summit lies over the more detached peaks to the north-west, Moel Eilio, Foel Gron and Moel Cynghorion. Far from the crowds, it adopts a switchback approach culminating in a prolonged climb above Clogwyn du'r Arddu to gain the Bwlch Glas. This upper section is also gained by a less demanding start from Snowdon Ranger youth hostel in Nant y Betws, a former inn that recalls a one-time mountain guide.

Pen-y-pass offers the most popular routes, aided by a starting altitude of 1180ft/360m. The direct routes follow either the Pyg Track or the Miners' Track into the folds of the mountain. The former starts an early climb to traverse the flanks of Crib Goch high above Llyn Llydaw, working efficiently round to meet the Miners' Track above the waters of Glaslyn. The broad, always animated Miners' Track rises cautiously to cross a causeway on Llyn Llydaw before climbing past mine workings to Glaslyn. The real climbing leads up to merge with the Pyg Track, and together they zigzag up to the Bwlch Glas between Snowdon and Crib y Ddysgl.

These approaches are outflanked by the ridges of Crib Goch and Y Lliwedd on either side - the Snowdon Horseshoe itself, and subject of the route described below. This is probably the finest mountain walk in the whole of England and Wales, and involves some rough going and delicate scrambling. The Crib Goch ridge is gained after a steep but very enjoyable climb from the Pyg Track

at Bwlch y Moch (Pass of the Pigs), to commence an airy traverse at around the 3000ft mark. The Crib Goch Pinnacles lead down to Bwlch Coch, and a prolonged climb leads onto Crib y Ddysgl.

For a clockwise approach, an ascent via Y Lliwedd sees the path break off the Miners' Track on reaching Llyn Llydaw. A rough slant up to the ridge precedes a grand crossing of the spiky top, after which a scrambly descent above dramatic cliffs works down to Bwlch y Ciliau, to meet the ascending Watkin Path.

ROUTE 21: SNOWDON & Y LLIWEDD

Summits:
Crib Goch   3028ft/923m
Crib y Ddysgl   3494ft/1065m
Snowdon   3560ft/1085m
Y Lliwedd   2946ft/898m

Start: Pen-y-pass (SH 647556). Car park on the summit of the pass, on the A4086 Llanberis-Capel Curig road. Seasonal Snowdon Sherpa bus from Llanberis, also from Beddgelert and Betws-y-Coed.

Distance: 7 miles/11km   **Ascent:** 4724ft/1440m

Maps:
OS 1:50,000 - Landranger 115. 1:25,000 - Outdoor Leisure 17

A path leaves the top of the upper car park, and at once the stately peak of Crib Goch throws down its challenge. With the Pass of Llanberis down to the right, the path works around the flank of the Horns then climbs to Bwlch y Moch. This proves to be a classic moment, looking across Llyn Llydaw to Y Lliwedd and Yr Wyddfa itself. At this major fork those overfaced by the prospect of Crib Goch can conveniently opt for the Pyg Track, which branches left over a ladder-stile to contour round the flank of the mountain.

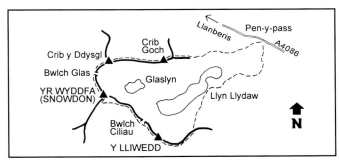

The Horseshoe route now sets about climbing in earnest, winding up to a shoulder then onto steeper ground where the first scrambling is encountered on inviting rock with ample holds. This relents for easier climbing up an arete to a cairn at the eastern end of Crib Goch: though not quite the summit, it provides the finest moment of the entire walk. Inspirationally revealed ahead is the horizontal arete leading past the summit to the menacing looking Pinnacles, with the ridge rising beyond to Crib y Ddysgl.

Commencing the crossing of Crib Goch, a bold traverse of the very crest is often shunned in favour of using it for handholds while picking a way along a shelf on the southern edge. This leads to the celebrated Pinnacles, and a largely obvious route through them. The second one features a short ledge on its left (south) side, leading to an airy notch. Across this gap the route climbs a more exposed shelf on the north, to gain increasingly easy ground. The roughness is vacated by descending onto the grassy Bwlch Coch, and normal walking leads towards Crib y Ddysgl. A gentle rise interrupted by a rocky knoll leads to the last real scrambling. An easy sloping crag is negotiated head-on, after which a narrow crest (or easier path to its north) leads a surprisingly extended climb onto the summit dome, crowned by an Ordnance Survey column.

Yr Wyddfa now awaits, its north-east face looking hugely impressive across Cwm Dyli. A short descent south-west leads around the rim of the cwm to Bwlch Glas. A finger of rock makes a welcome landmark in poor conditions, as the Llanberis path, railway line and Pyg/Miners' Tracks are met for a well populated final pull onto the summit of Wales. An Ordnance Survey column occupies a platform high above the cafe and its adjacent station.

Although the continuation to Y Lliwedd is south-east, a bee-line is not recommended as the ridge merely abuts onto Yr Wyddfa, rather than forming a practicable link. Instead, a brief descent south-west on the easy slopes towards Bwlch Main quickly reaches a grassy arrest of the ridge. A stone monolith sends a path slanting east, the roughness of this winter black-spot demanding caution at all times of the year.

The Snowdon Horseshoe from Llynnau Mymbyr, to the east
Opposite: Crib Goch from Snowdon; Moel Siabod beyond

Approaching Crib Goch from Pen-y-pass on a January morning

The stony path works down to Bwlch y Saethau, and a pleasant crossing to Bwlch Ciliau at the far side, where the Watkin Path departs for the valley. In front Y Lliwedd awaits, and the path scales the ridge with increasingly dramatic scenes unfolding on the left. This ascent is a perfect foil to the outward route, there being no menacing risks as an extended gentle scramble leads onto the summit. The first cairn marks the true crown, with a twin top a little beyond.

The descent works down past a lower eastern top before curving down through rockier terrain. Y Lliwedd's majestic crest towers behind, with Llyn Llydaw below. A cairn on a grassy shelf heralds the next stage of the descent, which is a rough slant down the northern spur towards the edge of the lake: Yr Wyddfa's mighty pyramid soars high above the waters. Just beyond a hut at the outflow, the Miners' Track is met fresh from crossing the causeway. This heads away for a relaxing conclusion as it sweeps round above Llyn Teryn and down to Pen-y-Pass.

MOEL HEBOG 2569ft/783m

Moel Hebog is a fine individual and highly accessible peak, towering in patriarchal fashion over the Alpine village of Beddgelert. This shapely hill sends a bumpy, high level ridge north to produce two further 2000ft peaks. Craggy slopes line the eastern rim of the summit, and these continue as the true northern ridge (Y Diffwys), a spur that curves down into Beddgelert Forest. The initially less interesting main ridge falls north-west to the Bwlch Meillionen, before proceeding over Moel yr Ogof and Moel Lefn. The addition of this pair creates a smashing circuit, a leisurely amble in summer and a challenging walk in winter's depths. Moel yr Ogof is named from a cave on its eastern flank, where it is claimed the Welsh hero Owain Glyndwr, descendent of the last native Prince of Wales, Llewelyn the Great, sought refuge.

By far the most frequented route onto the hill is a direct climb from Beddgelert, bracken pastures giving way to a typical ascent through scenes of increasing grandeur. In the upper stages the path weaves between craggier sections to gain the broad top. Starts can also be made from the popular Forestry Commission campsite in the extensive forest just north of the village. A public footpath climbs by the Afon Meillionen to escape the trees a little beneath the Bwlch Meillionen, from where a lengthy haul up the broad northern slopes awaits. Cwm Pennant offers few obvious routes, other than the corresponding western section of the path climbing to the Bwlch Meillionen.

A link to other high ground is forged at the Bwlch-y-Ddwy-elor, from where the delectable Nantlle Ridge strikes off to the south-west. A horseshoe of Cwm Pennant traversing both ridges would make a memorable outing, but whether included or not, the Nantlle Ridge makes a very positive contribution to a day on the Hebog ridge. It is preferable to walk north from Moel Hebog to Moel Lefn in order to savour everything at its finest, for in addition to the Nantlle Ridge ahead, the arresting Snowdon peaks rise to the right. Around these hills are numerous evidences of slate quarrying, the principal sites being found at either end of the ridge.

ROUTE 22: MOEL HEBOG

Summits:
Moel Hebog   2569ft/783m
Moel yr Ogof   2149ft/655m
Moel Lefn   2093ft/638m

Start: Beddgelert (SH 589481). Village car park. Served by Snowdon Sherpa bus from Caernarfon, Porthmadog and Llanberis.

Distance: 6½ miles/10½km   **Ascent:** 3050ft/930m

Maps:
OS 1:50,000 - Landranger 115. 1:25,000 - Outdoor Leisure 17

On the Porthmadog road a short back road turns up the side of the Royal Goat Hotel. As it bends left a public footpath rises to a few modern houses, but the route takes a gate on the right. A grassy track crosses the pasture to the site of the old railway station, and a little further, the grassy line is crossed to a gateway onto an old green way. This leads right, into trees to emerge via a stile and bridge onto Cwm Cloch Isaf farm road.

Above the farmhouse a track rises into trees and up to the house at Cwm Cloch Ganol. A stile sends a path slanting right across the pasture to sheepfolds at the far end. From a wall-stile to the right, the path slants left up a foxglove-filled pasture. Looking back, Cnicht and the Moelwyns are most impressive. At the top a cairn sends the path through an old wall, and a delightful grassy way climbs through bracken, steepening to a final stile at the top.

Moel Hebog from the Beddgelert path

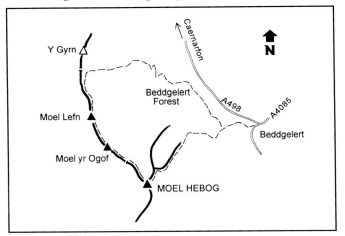

The summit of Moel Lefn, with the Nantlle Ridge beyond

Directly across, the Snowdon group, fronted by Yr Aran, increases in grandeur. The path enjoys a sustained, increasingly rough climb up the broad north-eastern ridge. Respite is earned on a shoulder, Y Grisiau, where it abuts onto the north ridge, a fine moment. Now it is but a short pull above a steep drop to the left to find an Ordnance Survey column alongside a wall.

The wall heading north-west guides an intermittent path down to Bwlch Meillionen. Across a crumbling wall in the narrow saddle the first stage of the re-ascent onto Moel yr Ogof is through a gash in gnarled bands of rock, above which a colourful pool is passed. As the wall turns away a thinner path continues up onto the top, delayed only momentarily by a false summit. Resuming north the path drops left out of modest bouldery slopes to a meeting of fence and wall. Beyond is a two-minute stroll to the bwlch and a brief pull onto Moel Lefn, whose summit overtops the first rocky boss encountered. Looking back, Moel Hebog appears a dark, surly character.

Continuing north along the broad top past another rocky boss, a thin path runs on to a very abrupt termination, revealing the finest view of the Nantlle Ridge. A winding path makes light work of the steep and craggier slopes down to Bwlch Sais, then resuming delightfully down easier ground. Ahead, the heathery knoll of Y Gyrn is prominent directly in front, as is the Jubilee Tower on Mynydd Tal-y-Mignedd on the Nantlle Ridge beyond. The path arrives with a little caution at the lip of a long abandoned hole at Princess Quarry, alongside the forest wall. From a make-shift stile a wallside path descends to Bwlch Cwm-trwsgl.

A stile gives access into the plantation, and a clear path drops down onto a forest road. Just 75 yards to the left a path delves back into the trees, and at a fork the right branch surprisingly emerges into daylight. The path undulates across colourful open country, and at a fork towards the end the left branch passes through moist terrain to a corner gate back into trees.

A charming path heads away, swinging down to the right to join a forest road; turning left, this winds down to a T-junction. To the right this runs steadily down before levelling out, with Moel Hebog looming large. Taking a lesser track doubling back left, a winding drive is joined to lead down to another level forest road. Turning right, this broad way swings down to accompany the Afon Meillionen. When the road swings away, a footpath continues straight down past lively falls to rejoin the road at a bridge. Crossing this the Beddgelert campsite is entered at a crossroads.

Advancing straight on, this broad way runs through the site to another crossroads towards the end. Straight on again and ignoring a branch right, it declines gently before running away from the campsite. Numerous clues point to this track's original purpose, the line of the Welsh Highland Railway. The line leads unfailingly on through woodland and clearings to meet the outward path at a stream that has lost its railway bridge. The track descends left to Cwm Cloch Isaf for Beddgelert.

MOEL SIABOD 2861ft/872m

As individual peaks go, they don't come much bigger and much more isolated than Moel Siabod. This fine mountain occupies an intriguing position on the edge of gentle, wooded country above Betws-y-Coed, yet is very much a part of the Snowdonia upland landscape. Indeed, there are few better vantage points for the great cirque of peaks from Snowdon to the Carneddau. Aloof, yet in the action, Moel Siabod towers to the south of Capel Curig from where it is invariably ascended.

The summit, Carnedd Moel Siabod, features an Ordnance Survey column overlooking slopes falling south to unfrequented country, while on the tilted plateau to its north is a large circular shelter built to coral early visitors' ponies. The mountain throws out characterful ridges to east and north-east, impounding a gem of a cwm containing the fair Llyn y Foel. Pick of these ridges is the shorter, no-nonsense eastern one, Daear Ddu. This bristly spur offers the perfect conclusion to an ascent route from the lake, which can be reached from two very different start points.

From Dolwyddelan in the Lledr Valley, a route ascends through extensive plantations before a path escapes to climb to Llyn y Foel. More popular is the route from Pont Cyfyng on the A5 to the north, which takes advantage of an old quarry road and later passes some absorbing remains of the abandoned industry. This neatly combines with the other standard route from Capel Curig, which climbs from Plas y Brenin through plantations onto the gentle northern slopes, for an easy angled and undemanding hike onto the upper reaches of the north-east ridge. This ridge could also be climbed in its entirety from where the Pont Cyfyng route gains the true base of the open hill, the path being generally clear as it scales heathery slopes.

Moel Siabod's link with other high ground is a rather tenuous one, utilising the meandering west ridge: beyond Clogwyn Bwlch-y-maen the spirited little peak of Y Cribau interrupts a decline to little more than a thousand feet before gnarled country re-ascends via Moel Meirch to the Moelwyns. Only the hardiest of walkers engage upon this crossing.

ROUTE 23: MOEL SIABOD

Summits:
Moel Siabod   2861ft/872m

Start: Capel Curig (SH 715578). Roadside parking on the A4086 Llanberis road immediately after Plas y Brenin. Seasonal Snowdon Sherpa buses from Bethesda, Llanberis, Betws-y-Coed and Llanwrst.

Distance: 6½ miles/10½km

Ascent: 2329ft/710m

Maps:
OS 1:50,000 - Landranger 115
1:25,000 -
Outdoor Leisure 17 & 18
(older version of sheet 17 covers the entire route)

Moel Siabod from Capel Curig

Adjacent to Plas y Brenin, a path runs down to a footbridge on the outflow from Llynnau Mymbyr. A forest road is followed east, past the house at Bryn-engan and along the base of the wood. Entering denser woodland the main way bears left, but a forest track keeps straight on to join the Afon Llugwy. The continuing path enjoys a beautiful walk downstream to Pont Cyfyng, passing en route a footbridge from Cobdens Hotel on the A5, then through an open pasture with Moel Siabod looming large to the right.

At the end the way is deflected across a sidestream, rising onto a drive. This joins the back road at Pont Cyfyng, a tall arched bridge spanning a fine gorge-like section of the river. Turning away from the bridge the cascades of the Cyfyng Falls are well seen over the wall.

At the first houses a private road bears right over a cattle-grid, climbing steeply to a hairpin bend where the diverted path bears left. This rises to rejoin the rough road above the farm at

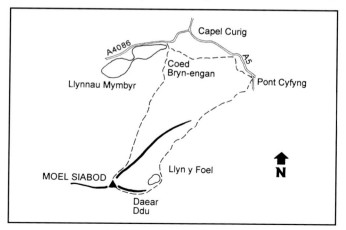

Rhos. At an abandoned farmhouse the open moor is gained, and looking back to the right, the Carneddau form a fine mountain group. This old quarry road rises effortlessly across the moor, with Moel Siabod waiting impressively ahead. Ignoring a branch left the track levels out at a gate/stile. From here a direct ascent of the main ridge could be made, the path being generally clear as it scales heathery slopes.

The track runs on to a reservoir, a lovely sheet of water in a colourful setting. A narrower path runs along its bank and climbs to the abandoned slate quarry above. The path ascends right of a spoil heap to enter the quarry area. Rising past ruins and up a former incline it arrives at the edge of a massive flooded hole. From above this a clear path leaves the site, quickly levelling out on a brow to reveal the finest moment of the walk, the Daear Ddu ridge seen climbing dramatically to the summit of the mountain. A few yards further and Llyn y Foel appears nestling in the cwm below. The path descends to its west side and rises to gain the foot of the ridge. An alternative route goes via the outflow, from where another path also crosses to the foot of the ridge.

The ridge can now be scaled in its entirety, a super path keeping as close as possible to the drop of the northern edge and seeking out any number of easy, optional scrambles. Half way up this lengthy but memorable climb, brief respite is found on a small knoll, looking both down the steep flank and up to fine crags on the upper slopes beneath our ridge. Views south look to Cnicht and the Moelwyns. The upper section offers no bouldery options until the final moments, when they return to divulge the summit environs, with the OS column just up to the left.

Descent begins by heading north past the old pony shelter, a thin path forming down the broad ridgetop. Though one could opt to remain on the stony ridge throughout its high level march, the more commonly used route breaks off it in the first shallow saddle before a minor re-ascent. Dropping left off the ridge through a few boulders, this return makes a near bee-line for the eastern end of Llynnau Mymbyr. A worn path forms immediately through the stones, and its rapid course down the grassy flank of the hill could not make a greater contrast with the ascent route.

Across gentler ground at the bottom the path drops to a stile in a fence junction, continuing down to the top corner of Coed Bryn-engan. Further down it swings into then back out of the wood to shadow a colourful stream, re-entering trees before slanting down onto a forest road. Approaching it, however, a short-cut path drops more directly onto it, and just a few yards left it takes off again through a clearing to meet the low-level forest road opposite Plas y Brenin.

Looking north along the Moel Siabod ridge

MOELWYN MAWR 2526ft/770m

The Moelwyn group of hills occupy a large tract of hugely colourful country between the celebrated Snowdon massif and the less enamouring slate quarries of Blaenau Ffestiniog. Almost all the summits form a horseshoe around the head of Cwm Croesor, with quarrying activity evident almost up to the summits of the main group.

Moelwyn Mawr stands to the southern edge of the group, with kid brother Moelwyn Bach to its south above the Vale of Ffestiniog. These two overlook the ugly concrete dam of Llyn Stwlan, forced to play its part in a hydro-electric storage scheme in an otherwise impressive cwm on the east side. To the west, gentler, less tarnished slopes fall towards Croesor. On Moelwyn Mawr's southern shoulder is the craggy bluff of Craigysgafn, which provides a sporting link between the two.

Though Moelwyn Mawr is the highest, all the tops are worth visiting, finest being the little outlier of Cnicht, universally known as the Welsh Matterhorn. Cnicht (the 'Knight') is only of modest altitude but remains one of the better known peaks, and its shapely aspect from the south makes it clear why. These walks are not all about bagging the highest tops, and if any walk deserved being extended to trawl some noteworthy surrounds, then Route 24 fully justifies the addition of Cnicht.

Another member of the group is Moel-yr-hydd, whose craggy eastern slopes overlook the quarries of Blaenau Ffestiniog. Greater interest is found in the two remarkable quarry holes that tenant the bwlch heading towards Moelwyn Mawr. These mighty craters are known as the East and West Twlls, and mark the upper limits of the remains of the once extensive Rhosydd Quarry. Slate was first won here more than 150 years ago, and at the peak of

Moelwyn Mawr and Moelwyn Bach across Cwm Croesor from Cnicht

ROUTE 24: MOELWYN MAWR

Summits:
Cnicht 2260ft/689m
Moel-yr-hydd 2126ft/648m
Moelwyn Mawr 2526ft/770m
Moelwyn Bach 2329ft/710m

Start: *Croesor (SH 631446). Car park in village centre. Served by bus from Porthmadog.*

Distance: *8½ miles/13½km*   **Ascent:** *3609ft/1100m*

Maps:
OS 1:50,000 - Landranger 115 & 124
1:25,000 - Outdoor Leisure 17 & 18

production gave employment to around 200 men. The greater of the remains, in the Bwlch y Rhosydd, include large barracks where the quarrymen would reside during the working week.

The northern half of the group includes the two summits of Ysgafell Wen, and also Moel Druman and Allt-fawr. The area leading to them is decorated by numerous attractive sheets of water, some of which were enlarged to provide water for the quarries.

For the principal peak, direct ascents are available from the minor road south of Croesor, either up the hill's west ridge, that of Moelwyn Bach, or the stream in between. The Ffestiniog side also offers unfrequented options, but these are outweighed by the charms of the western approaches. From Croesor an old miners' way slants up Cwm Croesor on the mountain's western flank to the former Croesor Quarry, and either on to Bwlch y Rhosydd or more directly up Moelwyn Mawr's north ridge. The adjacent Bwlch Cwmorthin can also be reached by an old quarry road from Tanygrisiau to the east, passing some extensive quarry remains and Llyn Cwmorthin.

From the car park entrance Cnicht rises majestically to fully justify its popular name, while the main Moelwyns are also well seen to the east. The road through the hamlet passes the school to climb steeply out, then descends to end at a fork of tracks. The cart track in front rises through woodland to level out on a brow. At a right fork Cnicht re-appears in grand style, while looking back there are already views to the estuary at Porthmadog. The track rises away, winding up to fade at a small ruin, where a grassy path climbs to a stile just above. This reveals the Moelwyns across the deep trough of Cwm Croesor, some time and distance away, as yet.

Henceforward the way is simple, heading up the wallside the path commences its ascent of Cnicht's delectable ridge. Cwm Croesor's various quarry remains include some sizeable inclines, while it is not long before the Snowdon peaks are revealed to the north. A gentle climb to a wall-stile under a rocky knoll precedes a traverse of a minor scree slope to a grassy col. Here the real ascent of the ridge begins, a sustained ladder of delights with some glorious views and rock often underfoot. Towards the top the path evades a large tilted slab, the upper section of which features an inviting optional scramble. Just above, appropriately, a small rock outcrop crowns the summit, a superb location with an attractive ridge continuing northwards to deny little Cnicht its true pyramid status.

The captivating view has numerous little lakes on display, with the lovely Llyn y Biswall close by. The Snowdon massif is pre-eminently arrayed, with the Glyders, the Carneddau and Moel Siabod all well seen; Moelwyn Mawr rises importantly above old quarry workings. Leaving most of Cnicht's visitors to retrace their ascent route, a path heads north along the ridge. Certainly at this stage the main Moelwyn tops appear entirely unrelated to Cnicht, but the transfer is far less demanding than anticipated. A thinner path runs by a couple of rocky tops before this gentler grassy ridge runs north-east to its low point just east of Llyn yr Adar.

At the far end of the broad saddle a cairn presides over a crossroads of ways, the main route turning right to effectively commence the second half of the walk. The largely clear path runs south-east on an undulating traverse through small hollows and over shoulders. Beyond a boulder field it runs gently on to pass above Llyn Cwm-corsiog. When the lake appears in near entirety from a brow, the path descends to a gate just short of its old dam. The path then drops down to Bwlch y Rhosydd, with Moelwyn Mawr looming large above the old quarry remains.

The heart of the former Rhosydd Quarry is entered, with the substantial remains of the barracks on the left, and lesser ruins of offices on the right. An incline rises away between the two, above the dark hole of an old adit issuing water. At the ruined drum house at the top the track bears left to undertake the same manoeuvre, this incline leading to a more open area. At the building in front a thin grassy path bears left, keeping spoil heaps and

ruins to its left. Approaching the dam of a drained reservoir, an area of spoil leads to a small stone hut where the site is vacated. A thin path rises south-east over grass to the summit of Moel-yr-hydd.

Though the top is unexceptional, it affords a sudden view of the Ffestiniog area, warts and all. The slate quarrying scene is rivalled by a power station by the large Tanygrisiau Reservoir at the very foot of the hill. More appealing is the brilliant prospect of the three Moelwyns, in particular the minor central peak, Craigysgafn.

Resuming west, a fence guides steps down to a saddle, with the East and West Twlls ahead. At the fence corner a thin trod bound directly for the West Twll meets a broad north-south path. A few yards to the left, a faint trod angles off to the edge of the West Twll, an amazing yawning chasm. From its top, grassy slopes rise to the rear of a rocky knoll, with a ladder-stile silhouetted in the skyline fence. Moelwyn Mawr's broad northern spur leads up above the cwm, with a path evident on the steeper section. Steady going at the grassy top leads to an unusual slate Ordnance Survey column, a stride from the steep drop.

Departing to the south-east, a path forms as the declivity to Craigysgafn is fully revealed, an impressive situation reminiscent of the rugged Rhinogs further south. The path winds pleasurably down to the saddle, then enjoys a lively traverse of Craigysgafn's intriguing rocky summit etched with quartz streaks. From a cairn at the end of this rugged little character, a cautious descent is made to Bwlch Stwlan.

At this crossroads a grassy track makes a direct return by heading west to omit Moelwyn Bach. This final peak presents an impregnable face to the bwlch, so the path rises briefly from the crossroads before taking evasive action by slanting up a slaty scree slope. It doubles back to ease out at a cairn before a gentle rise onto the summit plateau. The cairn stand a little to the left of two outcrops of curiously angled slabs.

Heading west, a path soon forms for a delectable downhill stride, a perfect conclusion on a summer's evening. Ahead, the rivers Glaslyn and Dwyryd merge at the estuary at Porthmadog. Looking back, smashing little Craigysgafn is seen under Moelwyn Mawr, and the distinctive profile of the Moelwyns' very own 'Grey Man' might be revealed beneath Moelwyn Bach's summit.

As the path fades towards the bottom, a path from the bwlch is found to the right. This flounders in boggy ground before the plantation corner ahead, where a gate admits to the forest. A path heads away along its edge, and part way on it angles into the trees for a lovely stroll out onto a back road. This emerges from the trees to divulge a glorious prospect, with Cnicht and the Moelwyns illuminating a traffic-free return to the village.

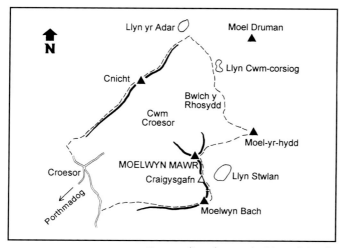

Descending the south ridge of Cnicht

ARENIG FAWR   2802ft/854m

Arenig Fawr is highest of a disparate group of hills rising to the north and west of Bala. It stands head and shoulders above these independent summits rising to the north above the sweeping moors of the Migneint. Travelling from Bala to Trawsfynydd, the fast shoreline road by Llyn Celyn reveals the hill's shapely eastern profile, and with it more than enough temptation to get out and climb it. George Borrow's mid-19th century wanderings in *Wild Wales* induced this accolade: 'Of all the hills which I saw in Wales none made a greater impression upon me'. A kid brother Arenig Fach rises directly across the main road, and is very much a scaled down version, even to the smaller lake its lesser crags overlook.

Arenig Fawr's stature may be diminished somewhat by the fact that it crowns rolling moorlands that are already high above sea level. It is, nevertheless, a big mountain, and a fine one. Its two major scenes of interest are a craggy lower eastern face, and a broad summit plinth. The former is centred on Llyn Arenig Fawr: enlarged to form a reservoir which feeds Llyn Celyn, it makes a fine foreground to the craggy slopes behind.

The summit is known as Moel yr Eglwys ('Rounded Hill of the Church'), and incorporates an Ordnance Survey column, a cairn of ancient pedigree now of use as a shelter, and a memorial to the crew of an American Flying Fortress which crashed here in 1943. The short-lived summit ridge extends south to incorporate a minor top before falling to a pool-strewn plateau. On a clear day eyes are largely focused on the great skyline of mountains to the west, where the nearest peaks are the line-up of Rhinogs and the cluster of Moelwyns. To the south the high ridge of the Arans also rises conspicuously.

The scattered hamlet of Arenig, on a minor road to the south of Llyn Celyn, is the natural starting point for ascents, a route which was more popular when Bala-Ffestiniog trains would deposit eager visitors at Arenig station: sadly a scene very difficult to imagine today. The first objective is Llyn Arenig Fawr, from where the real ascent begins, usually to the southern rim of the crags on Y Castell (The Castle). The upper slopes then prove quite gentle, with only minor outcrops featuring beneath the summit dome.

Ascents from the south are based on the moorland road that climbs from Llanuwchllyn towards Trawsfynydd, a likely route including the neighbouring 2464ft/751m Moel Llyfnant. From the east, around Maestron, paths set out across rough pastures to gain open moorland leading to the steep southern slopes of the summit area. Llyn Arenig Fawr could also be reached from the moorland road west of Llidiardau.

ROUTE 25: ARENIG FAWR

Summits:
Arenig Fawr   2802ft/854m

Start: Arenig (SH 834393). Roadside start by the phone box on a back road south of Llyn Celyn. Occasional buses run along the nearby A4212 Bala-Trawsfynydd road. A notice advises that dogs are excluded at lambing time.

Distance: 7 miles/11km   **Ascent:** 1854ft/565m

Maps:
OS 1:50,000 - Landranger 125
1:25,000 - Outdoor Leisure 18

At the next house east along the road a gate accesses a waymarked courtesy path on the Bala-Ffestiniog railway. The grassy line passes through a cutting before an old station house forces a brief detour back onto the road. Back on track, an embankment offers big views over Llyn Celyn before a drive from Boch-y-Rhaeadr joins the old trackbed. When this turns up onto the road, it is necessary to double back 300 yards to a parking verge, where a Landrover track climbs away from a gate on the south side.

The track eases out to run south across the moor before descending to Llyn Arenig Fawr, with Arenig Fawr now being far better appraised. The track ends near a small stone hut that is currently maintained as a bothy. From the adjacent kissing-gate a thin path crosses the outflowing stream and then makes for the foot of the waiting ridge. A delightful climb leads up through the colourful vegetation of this grassy shoulder overlooking the lake. It steepens towards the top to a makeshift stile in a fence abutting onto the rocky bluff of Y Castell.

The path resumes above at a gentler gradient to another fence corner. Going left with it briefly, another makeshift stile sees the path over the fence and slanting left, to then contour above a hollow before landing on a moist shelf. Across it the path slants south-west as it sets about the upper slopes, and virtually levels out for some time across the face of the hill. Becoming only a fainter trod at its highest point, a defined spur of stony outcrops and several small cairns confirm this as the moment to depart. Initially steep slopes lead onto easier grass, from where a short rise gains the main ridge of the hill.

The route returns to this point after visiting the summit, which stand further south-west. An intermittent path is guided by old fence posts along the broad ridge. In mist a couple of false tops present themselves, but the main one is unmistakeable as a short, stony haul gains the well defined cone, surmounted by the OS column and shelter with its slate memorial.

Returning north-east, the minor tops are passed to quickly rise onto a modest grassy top. Just beyond its cairn the ridge forks, each branch carrying remnants of the old fence. The north-west branch passes initially above a minor scarp on the left, though the main hazard is stray fence wire. The way descends gently to a cairned end, then more steeply on a thin path with sweeping westerly views. Approaching a wall corner, its north side leads down to level out before a small marsh defends a firm track.

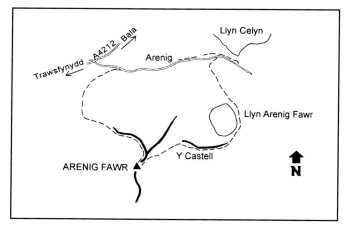

This public footpath leads northwards for a pleasant stroll to a set of sheepfolds under a canopy of trees. Passing to their left the Landrover track heads away, but the grassy embankment of the parallel former railway line offers a nicer stroll. Just short of the road it meets an impasse, so the track must be rejoined for the final yards. The quiet road leads back past a large quarry site and also the site of Arenig Station to finish.

CADAIR BERWYN 2723ft/830m

The Berwyn Mountains lay claim to a vast tract of rolling upland in the heart of Wales, from above the shores of Llyn Tegid (Bala Lake) almost to Llangollen. Largely excluded from the Snowdonia National Park, they are also far removed from accepted mountain walking country. In truth, much of the Berwyn is unexciting heather-clad moorland, where long, arduous miles of tramping are the preserve of the solitary walker who thrives on such terrain. There is, however, just one locality where dramatic scenery comes to the fore, where the exceptional Pistyll Rhaeadr plunges beneath the highest peaks. Translation of the waterfall into English reveals some excessive duplication!

These summits are without question the crowning glory of Berwyn country, forming a high-level ridge falling to deep cwms. The main peak is Cadair Berwyn, which with its partner Moel Sych overlooks the finest of the cwms. This is occupied by Llyn Lluncaws, an archetypal mountain pool set in a perfect hanging valley. The third principal top is the outlying high peak of Cadair Bronwen. 'Bronwen's Chair' offers itself for an out and back stride to boost a steady ramble over the high Berwyn to an appreciable yet still undemanding day on the hills.

All the summit cairns on the main ridge are indicated on maps as meriting antiquity status, while remains of mysterious stone circles and rows pepper the vast slopes of the hills. To the east of the main ridge, lower, gentle ridges parallel each other, all penetrated by cul-de-sac lanes serving peacefully secreted farmsteads from cosy little villages. Westwards, shorter valleys fall to the upper reaches of the Dee, and the characterful settlements of Llandrillo, Cynwyd and Corwen.

Pistyll Rhaeadr, the highest waterfall in Wales

On Cadair Berwyn

ROUTE 26: CADAIR BERWYN

Summits:
Cadair Berwyn   2723ft/830m
Cadair Bronwen   2575ft/785m
Moel Sych   2713ft/827m

Start: *Pistyll Rhaeadr (SJ 074294). Four miles north-west of Llanrhaeadr-ym-Mochnant. Car park and cafe at the road-end at Tan-y-pistyll, and lay-bys just before that. Llanrhaeadr has infrequent buses from Oswestry.*

Distance: 7½ miles/12km   **Ascent:** 2582ft/787m

Maps:
OS 1:50,000 - Landranger 125. 1:25,000 - Explorer 255

Far and away the best route onto the high tops begins at Tan-y-pistyll, in the shadow of the famous waterfall. An old track, now a grassy delight, runs above the Nant y Llyn to Llyn Luncaws, and the east ridge of Moel Sych is a direct route onto the summit ridge. Cadair Berwyn is then an easy half-mile walk to the north. Moel Sych's south ridge is another good route, with colourful lower slopes looking into the upland valley of the Afon Disgynfa.

For easier access, a longer stride can be enjoyed from Llandrillo to the north-west, where an easy angled old drovers' way slants across the sprawling flank of Cadair Bronwen to gain the main ridge at Bwlch Maen Gwynedd. Also, a horseshoe walk of Cwm Maen Gwynedd from the east makes for a longer spell on the tops - and more summits. Finally, a long skyline march from Moel Fferna to the north, or the B4391 Llangynog-Bala road at Milltir Gerrig to the south, will ensure a fuller appreciation of Berwyn country.

At the car park entrance a path climbs to the right between old walls and into trees. A gate on the left gives access to the wood beneath the falls, for an early appraisal of Pistyll Rhaeadr. The continuing path quickly leaves the trees to emerge into the open country of the Nant y Llyn. The main path is immediately forsaken, with the object of gaining a broad path on the opposite slope. Turning down to cross a wide grassy track, a thinner green way slants down to cross the stream. Up the other bank a path doubles back through bracken to rise onto the inviting old way.

Rising gently across bracken slopes this is a classic stride: Cadair Berwyn is high above, with views back to the upper part of the falls. Limestone outcrops feature, with evidence of lead mining across the valley. At an early fork the uphill branch maintains its steady rise, ultimately crossing the stream. Soon shadowing the outflow from Llyn Lluncaws, within minutes of crossing it the path approaches the rim of the cwm, with the lake just ahead.

While a thin path advances to the water's edge, the main path turns to tackle the steep east ridge of Moel Sych enclosing the cwm. This super climb on a largely grassy path sees the lake

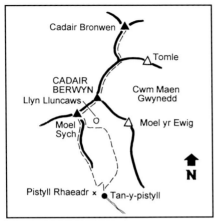

In the valley of the Nant y Llyn, en route to Moel Sych. The ascent path towards Llyn Lluncaws can be seen on the opposite flank, on the slopes of Moel yr Ewig

featuring strongly in grand views. At the top Moel Sych's nearby summit can be by-passed for now, as the rim of the cwm makes a very short drop to the saddle with Cadair Berwyn. A path rises to its beckoning peak, crossing a stile just short of the jagged top.

The summit claims an enviable location overlooking two side valley heads, and though not obviously the top from a glance at the map, it clearly is when stood upon it. While the return route is back over Moel Sych, a promenade north along the high-level crest is recommended, first passing a large circular shelter and a pool in a saddle to reach the Ordnance Survey column that was long assumed to be the summit. A good mile and a half further stands Cadair Bronwen, the group's third 2500-footer, though if not opting for that, then the short half-mile along the crest of Craig Berwyn is still strongly recommended. As Craig Berwyn relents, the ridge twists north-west for the path to descend to Bwlch Maen Gwynedd before a short pull to Cadair Bronwen's massive cairn.

Back on Cadair Berwyn, a return to its southern col leads to a short rise to a fence junction and cairn on the summit of Moel Sych. The left-hand fence encourages a path to shadow it down the south ridge, with fine views back over to Cadair Berwyn from nearer the edge. When the fence ends an inviting path continues down the moorland pasture, culminating in bracken at the bottom of the Afon Disgynfa valley. In addition to hearing the waterfall, the fine cliffs just across its ravine are well seen. Just below, a stile accesses a natural viewing platform at the top of the waterfall, where a degree of caution must be exercised. Back on the hill, a grassy path turns east to re-enter the Nant y Llyn valley.

Very soon a path breaks off to wind a steep, zigzag course down the slopes, rejoining the outward route at the edge of the trees. Returning to Pistyll Rhaeadr, a small footbridge makes a splendid viewing station on the stream beneath the falls. From here another path runs downstream to re-enter the car park alongside the cafe verandah in its Alpine setting.

ARAN FAWDDWY 2969ft/905m
GLASGWM 2559ft/780m

The Aran Hills are an enigmatic mountain group, the axis being a long, high-level ridge running north-south from Llanuwchllyn at the head of Llyn Tegid (Bala Lake), to Dinas Mawddwy. The lofty crest of the ridge has three peaks above 2850ft, and various other summits to their south. The ridge conforms to a simple pattern, as gentle western slopes contrast with plunging eastern flanks. The ridge also spawns further summits to the east, and though these rolling hills offer the best views of the main mountains, they are a world apart from the peaks, crags and cwms of the principal ridge.

The major peak is Aran Fawddwy, the highest mountain in Britain south of Snowdon. This majestic hill is in the thick of the action: from its very summit an untamed eastern flank falls to the exquisitely situated Creiglyn Dyfi. This gem of a pool is the source of the Afon Dyfi (River Dovey). To the north the ridge rumbles on over the two other highest peaks, Erw y Ddafad-ddu and Aran Benllyn, while to the south its curving arms diverge as the ridge stumbles on less purposefully to resurrect itself on Glasgwm, more than two miles distant.

Appearing as one of the less innocuous of the Welsh 2500-footers, Glasgwm nevertheless shows a mightily impressive face to Cwm Cywarch, where the dark cliffs of Craig Cywarch hover steeply and menacingly. Glasgwm also claims its own sheet of water, the elevated Llyn y Fign. Here too the ridge splits again, one branch crossing the summit of Pen y Brynfforchog (2247ft/685m) to the Ochr y Bwlch. The more attractive one runs south-east over shapely Y Gribin, which just fails to reach 2000ft, and Foel Benddin above Dinas Mawddwy.

Aran Fawddwy from Llechwedd Du, to the east

Access to the Aran peaks is a sensitive issue, with paths negotiated between the National Park Authority and landowners. Notices at access points warn that no dogs are allowed, and that renewal of these 'concessions' depends on our reasonable use. Not all the routes listed on the approach notices are marked as such on the Outdoor Leisure map (1998 edition). To cause further confusion, most of the concession routes begin as public rights of way, even though they don't reach the summits as such.

This very unsatisfactory business does raise an anomaly: as most hill farmers seem to receive grants and subsidies to enable them to survive (and reasonably so, if they are looking after the countryside), then we taxpayers are paying them to keep us off the hills! For the record, these are the permitted access points, with grid references: Llanuwchllyn 880297; Cwm onen 863279; Esgair-gawr 815223; Lletty-wyn 813217; Cwm Cwarch 853187; Ochr y Bwlch 803170.

By far the finest approach to either of the two object peaks is from Cwm Cywarch to the south. For Aran Fawddwy, the pre-eminent route is the path slanting above the deep fold of Hengwm to a bwlch south of Drysgol, then rising over Drysgol and Drws Bach onto the main peak's rugged southern flank. The most direct route to Glasgwm is the path which makes an enthralling climb up an inviting cwm directly beneath its craggy flank, and from the bwlch north of the summit it scales the engaging north-eastern slopes onto the broad top.

The most obvious alternative is the ridge concession path from the north. This begins at Llanuwchllyn at the head of Llyn Tegid. At Pont y Pandy a farm road sees the way off, and moving onto a bridleway the concession path soon materialises as open country is gained. The long, steady climb to Aran Benllyn increases in interest as the ridge proper forms, and craggy flanks fall to the pool of Llyn Lliwbran. The disadvantage of this route is a dearth of variations for the return.

A truly beautiful approach would be from Llanymawddwy to the south-east, where a public footpath runs into Cwm Dyniewyd, a colourful scene dominated by the remarkable valley head waterfall of Pistyll Gwyn. At the amphitheatre a well-made path slants up steep flanks, rising above the lovely waterslides to terminate at an upper fall. Unfortunately the right of way also ends here: there is no official 'concession' link, as there quite obviously should be, for the missing mile to the similarly cul-de-sac public footpath rising from Hengwm to the bwlch south of Drysgol. However an obvious line traces the Afon Pumryd outside a plantation and on up to the bwlch.

Bwlch y Groes makes a high-level start point from the east, and though seemingly distant the Arans ridge presents a splendid front. However, several lesser tops and the Bwlch Sirddyn intervene, as does the access agreement. The bwlch carries a public footpath linking Talardd in the north with Pennant in the south,

Aran Benllyn and Creiglyn Dyfi from Drysgol

and above it the ridge of Foel Hafod-fynydd (2260ft/689m) is a short steep climb. From its quartz cairned top the eastern face of the Arans ridge beckons even stronger when 'forbidden'. It is to be hoped that access will soon be restored to some of these routes.

At the very southern terminus of the ridge, the A470 road summit on Ochr y Bwlch gives a good high-level start, taking in Pen y Brynfforchog en route to Glasgwm, easy fence-side walking above the head of a plantation. This would also be the logical start point for a true end-to-end traverse of the ridge. Approaches from the west commence at either Esgair-gawr or Lletty-wyn on a minor road just off the A494 near Rhydymain. Though starting within half a mile of each other and both ascending through the dark plantations of Coed-y-Brenin, they offer different routes onto the main ridge, one reaching the bwlch beneath Glasgwm, the other further north on the upper slopes of Aran Fawddwy itself.

ROUTE 27: ARAN FAWDDWY & GLASGWM

Summits:
Aran Fawddwy   2969ft/905m
Erw y Ddafad-ddu   2861ft/872m
Aran Benllyn   2904ft/885m
Glasgwm   2559ft/780m

Start: Cwm Cywarch (SH 853184). A recognised parking area at the end of a patch of open ground just short of the road end in Cwm Cywarch. This is some two miles along a cul-de-sac road leaving the minor road to Bwlch y Groes, immediately after the bridge one mile east of Dinas Mawddwy (A470). Dinas Mawddwy is served by bus from Machynlleth and Dolgellau.

Distance: 11½ miles/18½ km (8½/13½ omitting the two northern peaks)

Ascent: 3861ft/1177m (3313ft/1010m omitting the two northern peaks)

Maps:
OS 1:50,000 - Landranger 124 or 125. 1:25,000 - Outdoor Leisure 23

A little further along the road, a footbridge sends a green way off, narrowing as it climbs between hedgerows. After a brief kink it slants more steeply left, now a broader green way which sets the tone for a well graded ascent. Superb views look over the cirque of Hengwm, while further back is the deep-cut side valley of the descent route. Reverting to footpath width beyond a stream, this old path slants uniformly across the flank of Pen yr Allt Uchaf. Prominent on the valley floor is a large quartz 'compass', while on the skyline high above is a cairn on Drws Bach. Arriving on a peaty bwlch at 1873ft/571m, the path swings left to begin a more traditional climb, rising close by a fence to a stile at the top. This prized moment heralds the stunning appearance of the uppermost craggy contours of Aran Fawddwy.

The path swings left along the southern edge of Drysgol, whose minor summit, at 2444ft/745m, sits just to the north. A brief spell above the precipitous grassy slopes falling to Hengwm leads to a narrowing of the ridge, with the memorial cairn on Drws Bach beckoning. By now the full grandeur of Aran Fawddwy is revealed, its craggy face falling into the waters of Creiglyn Dyfi. Resuming, the landmark cairn on Drws Bach proves to occupy a remarkable location, the finest of the walk. It pays tribute to a young member of St. Asaph Mountain Rescue Team, who tragically perished near here after being struck by lightning during an exercise in 1960. A metal box protects a visitor's book.

Though a slender path goes left down the arete towards Gwaun y Llwyni (2247ft/685m), Aran Fawddwy awaits, and the main path shadows a fence round to a stile at the foot of the steep slope. In poor conditions the fence makes a reliable guide, though it is rather less interesting than tracing a sketchy path directly up the stony flank, easing out at a cairned top before crossing to the Ordnance Survey column. Astride a massive pile of stones, the trig. point enjoys a fine prospect down the eastward declivity, with plenty of boulders to offer shelter. If following the fence, a junction is reached en route to a bend where the fence goes off left. From here a gentle rise leads onto the summit crest. Perhaps the pick of this grand view is westward, where the Cadair Idris range looks especially shapely.

The enticing prospect northwards to the two further 2500-footers encourages a high altitude extension, commencing with an improving path descending the stony north slopes to a pair of stiles and an old wall in the bwlch. The fence offers a foul weather alternative to the crest, on which very easy walking leads to the less glamorous top of Erw y Ddafad-ddu. A cairn sits atop a broad grassy plinth, to the north of which a minor knob affords a better prospect into the valley and ahead to the greater appeal of Aran Benllyn.

The fence leads northwards again, dropping to a minor col from where a decent path crosses to its west side. Re-crossing at the final stile precedes a gentle pull to the summit of Aran Benllyn. An old wall runs across the top, with the cairn sat immediately through it. Dazzling bands of quartz erupt immediately north and south of the summit, just yards from which a stupendous craggy drop can be viewed.

Back on Aran Fawddwy, the fence leads southwards to its upper junction. The western arm makes a direct descent, initially stony but then through a grassy bowl onto boggier ground. A chain of planks make light of the crossing of the moorland crest of Waun Camddwr to drop to the bwlch under Glasgwm. Marker posts shun

Walkers approaching the Glasgwm bwlch, with Aran Fawddwy and Gwaun y Llwyni behind

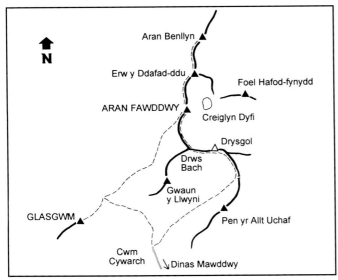

sharp bends in the fence, taking the path directly across the saddle to another fence. It is from this cross-fence that the final descent will commence. For Glasgwm however, a stile in a fence junction to the right sends a grand path to shadow the steeply climbing fence. It eases in the upper half to level out on Glasgwm's top. A solid, pyramid-shaped cairn awaits, overlooking the tiny Llyn Bach on the right. Llyn y Fign is only revealed on touching the cairn, a substantial pool to occupy a summit. To the west are Rhobell Fawr and Ddualt with the shapely Rhinogs skyline further back.

Back at the bwlch a classic descent begins, fading yellow arrows painted on strategic rocks aiding this occasionally sketchy path. Every step is a delight as the way winds down the upper side valley, enjoying views of waterfalls in the ravine. Lower down it crosses a footbridge to slant down through bracken, with a frowning crag above. A great boiler plate rock is passed before a stile onto a rough road by some old mine workings. Turning right, a right fork approaches the farm at Blaencywarch, whose surfaced access road leads rapidly back to the start.

CADAIR IDRIS 2930ft/893m

Cadair Idris is one of the most popular and highly respected mountains in Wales, a compact massif of summits, crags, ridges and especially delectable mountain lakes. Its long, frowning skyline forms a dark wall set high above the town of Dolgellau, and it earns further merits in its stance over the Mawddach estuary.

The summit is known as Penygadair, a rocky, characterful place as befits this famous peak. A novel feature and a reminder of more eccentric times is a stone-built refuge, erected when Cadair Idris was usually ascended with the aid of a mountain guide. While the summit may appear reasonably hospitable, the pattern of this mountain differs from most in that extremely craggy slopes fall away both north and south. While the latter are less immediate, they emphasise the fact that escape routes are largely limited to the recognised ascent lines.

This principal peak rises between two outstanding lake-filled cwms. Idris was a character of disputed legendary pedigree, and his 'Chair' is the great northern cwm. Cwm Cau, to the south, contains a larger sheet of water: Llyn Cau virtually fills this deep hollow, and the surrounding cliffs rise oppressively above its shores. Cwm Cau and these south-eastern flanks of the hill form the Cadair Idris National Nature Reserve, a refuge of rare arctic-alpine plants.

The magnificent northern escarpment extends for several miles, overlooking a series of cwms and cliffs that together form a near impenetrable barrier. The tops of Mynydd Moel, Gau Graig and Cyfrwy all occupy airy positions above these craggy flanks. The western ridge continues less dramatically for some time, re-claiming a 2000ft altitude over two further summits with even better prospects over the mouth of the Mawddach at Barmouth. Even beyond these, sprawling hills advance further to the coast.

There are two principal ascent lines, from north-west and south-east. The latter is a start from Minffordd near the attractive lake of Tal-y-llyn, a route short on mileage but brimfull of everything else: this horseshoe of Cwm Cau also encompasses the two other main summits of the group, Craig Cwm Amarch and Mynydd Moel. A variation on this, direct if less appealing, is to continue on a branch path to Llyn Cau, and from the very head of the cwm a rough path climbs steeply out between craggy flanks to gain the saddle above Craig Cau for the final pull to the summit. Less well defined in ascent is this horseshoe's return leg, which involves crossing Nant Cadair after emerging from the trees, and scaling a grassy rib to the gentler upper slopes of Mynydd Moel.

Similarly short and popular are ascents from the minor road to the north, near Llyn Gwernan above Dolgellau. Most direct is the Fox's Path, which takes in the pools of Llyn Gafr and Llyn y Gadair before a very steep haul out of the upper cwm to gain the summit: its popularity however has been its undoing, for such is the eroded condition of the interminable loose scree of its steep, higher reaches that its use is rightly discouraged. A little longer and less demanding is the Pony Path, commencing from a car park near Ty-Nant, west of Llyn Gwernan: this was a favourite route in Victorian times, climbing to a bwlch with the outlying Tyrrau Mawr before scaling the western shoulder of Cyfrwy to gain the rim of the awesome Llyn y Gadair cwm.

A splendid long stride from Llanfihangel-y-pennant to the south-west is the southerly continuation of the popular Pony Path, and this variant remains a bridleway throughout its length. Finally, an ascent from the north-east would cross the outlying summit of Gau Graig, to enjoy a steady climb above the northern edges - and the unfrequented little Llyn Arran - to arrive on the summit acres by way of Mynydd Moel.

Right: Cadair Idris from the north

ROUTE 28: CADAIR IDRIS

Summits:
Craig Cwm Amarch   2595ft/791m
Cyfrwy   2661ft/811m
Cadair Idris   2930ft/893m
Mynydd Moel   2f831t/863m

Start: Minffordd (SH 731116). National Park Dôl Idris car park by the junction of A487 (Dolgellau-Machynlleth) and B4405 to Tywyn. Served by Dolgellau-Machynlleth buses.

Distance: 6½ miles/10½km   **Ascent:** 2970ft/905m

Maps:
OS 1:50,000 - Landranger 124. 1:25,000 - Outdoor Leisure 23

From the end of the car park a broad path runs through an avenue of horse chestnut trees, deflecting left to the Ystradlyn Visitor Centre. A short way left along the track, across a bridge on Nant Cadair, a kissing-gate sees the climb begin. The path makes an immediately steep start through beautiful woods, further enlivened by cascades on the adjacent stream. The going eases at an old iron gate, and the trees fall away to give views back over the valley.

The path runs on, nearing the stream at the top of a pine-wood opposite. Climbing gently, the surrounds open out to reveal the prospect of the rough southern slopes of Mynydd Moel. Rising to a plateau, the full grandeur of Cwm Cau is appraised, with Cadair Idris to the right, and the first top, Craig Cwm Amarch, to the left. At a massive cairn the way forks, the right branch tempting a few minutes' stroll past a large tilted slab to the shore of Llyn Cau.

The left branch makes a sustained pull on a pitched path to gain the ridge top, and swings right for an uncomplicated scamper up the enclosing arm of the cwm leading to Craig Cwm Amarch. A rocky ridge often shields the path from the abrupt edge, though

113

more sporting options are available. Heady views look down the clefts into the cwm, then a plateau precedes the final pull onto the summit, marked by the arrival of a fence.

Across the stile the path is initially faint as the broad ridge makes a short drop northwards to the col. Meeting the head of the direct path from the cwm, a straightforward climb to the summit of Cadair begins. Part way up, it is more rewarding in clear weather to veer left to meet the main ridge rising from the west. Just before the edge the broad Pony Path is met. Gaining the craggy edge is a profound moment, and with it a chance to detour around the cirque to the top of Cyfrwy. This offers a fine prospect of the principal peak rising across the waters of Llyn y Gadair.

A shelter and cairn stand aloof from the mainstream ways, making this a place to relax and take in the prospect of the final miles of the Mawddach, leading to the estuary, bridge and sands at Barmouth. Another fine view is south-west into the Dysynni valley, with Craig yr Aderyn (Birds' Rock) prominent. Returning along the edge, the Pony Path scales the final slopes to the waiting Ordnance Survey column on Penygadair, summit of Cadair Idris. Just beneath it to the north is the amply proportioned stone refuge.

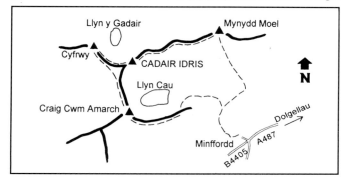

Cyfrwy and Llyn y Gadair from Cadair Idris

Heading eastwards, the initial descent on a modest path offers the easiest walking of the route, passing the emergence, marked by twin cairns, of the Fox's Path. Past a stony cairned top (852m) overlooking the edge, the way strides pleasantly on and gradually down to a col before a gentle rise. In mist a cairn on a rocky knoll suggests itself as the summit of Mynydd Moel, but a fence-stile 50 yards further precedes a brief pull to the rocks of the summit, marked by a cairn and shelter.

The presence of the fence renders the descent infallible, with easy grassy slopes leading south-eastwards to steeper, stonier sections. The views down to the valley are increasingly supplanted by the improving prospect of Cwm Cau. Eventually an old wall corner is passed through, and further down, after a wall goes left, a stile sends a path slanting right, through yet another old wall to the stream at the head of the pine forest, with the outward path on the opposite bank.

WAUN FACH 2661ft/811m

The Black Mountains form the eastern outpost of the peaks of Wales, indeed they spill over into the valleys of Herefordshire. One mountain summit stands on the very border, a status shared only with Windy Gyle on the England-Scotland border ridge. Only two summits breach the 2500ft mark, and within a mile of each other Pen y Gadair Fawr ('Top of the Big Chair') plays grudging support to its inferior patriarch, Waun Fach ('Little Moor'). After enjoying the suggested excursion, it will readily be appreciated that the summit of a walk can be the least interesting point, so there's a lesson for obsessive peak-baggers!

The Black Mountains provide long, broad ridges made for long, broad strides at high level. Deep valleys penetrate between steep flanks, none better than the Vale of Ewyas, in which Llanthony Priory and Capel-y-ffin are secreted. Only at the northern edge do these hills present an escarpment, a less demonstrative one than those of the two main groups to the west. Waun Fach fails to get involved in this scarp business, though it does occupy a pivotal position sending two high ridges south. Cwms and spurs to the west present the hill's best side, where the superior Y Grib ridge, the 'Dragon's Back', climbs above the ancient fort of Castell Dinas.

Waun Fach is most easily reached from Pengenfford on the crest of the Crickhowell-Talgarth road. Paths over Y Grib or up Rhiw Trumau both find attractive surroundings, to be followed by undemanding sections on the hill's upper contours. Most obvious alternative route is to make Waun Fach the turning point of a big horseshoe walk of the Grwyne Fechan valley, based on the little village of Llanbedr, near Crickhowell. This carries the advantage of traversing Pen y Gadair Fawr in addition to the appealing Pen Allt Mawr on the western of the two ridges, and allows one to remain above the 2000ft contour for an exceptional distance. Waun Fach can also be easily reached by a very high level start from the top of the Gospel Pass road linking the Vale of Ewyas with Hay-on-Wye, passing over Twmpa and Rhos Dirion: it does however offer less scope for an alternative return route.

ROUTE 29: WAUN FACH

Summits:
Waun Fach   2661ft/811m
Pen y Gadair Fawr   2625ft/800m

Start: Pengenfford (SO 173296). Start from the Castle Inn on the A479 Crickhowell road, three miles south of Talgarth. A small fee is payable for use of the car park. Talgarth is served by Brecon-Hereford buses.

Distance: 10½ miles/17km (8 miles/13km omitting Pen y Gadair Fawr)

Ascent: 2346ft/715m (2018ft/615m omitting Pen y Gadair Fawr)

Maps:
OS 1:50,000 - Landranger 161. 1:25,000 - Outdoor Leisure 13

Behind the car park alongside the pub, a path is signed down an old hedgerowed byway. Only a short way down, a stile sends a permitted path down a fieldside to cross a tiny stream, followed by a stiff pull up fieldsides to gain the grassy ramparts of Castell Dinas. The banks of this dramatically sited Iron Age hillfort enclose the scant remains of a Norman castle, though it is the older fortification that gives the site its character. All this and views too, the shapely ridge of Y Grib ridge contrasting with the great sprawl of Waun Fach.

Descending north-east, a stile gives access to the saddle with the connecting ridge. Easiest option is to resume straight up the spur, over a minor top to Bwlch Bach a'r Grib. Alternatively, a cart track runs along the northern base, and as it drops away a path contours round to meet a rising bridleway offering another brief choice of routes. The gentlest way slants up the flank of Y Grib to join the ridge beyond the modest outcrops, though it is preferable to double back right up this grassy bridleway to gain the ridge at Bwlch Bach a'r Grib. This reveals a fine prospect southwards down the Rhiangoll valley.

The crest of the ridge is an infallible guide as it climbs through the small outcrops of Y Grib. Looking back, the assertive peaks of the Brecon Beacons rise beyond Mynydd Troed. The rocks expire before an isolated cairn is reached, at which point the leg-work is complete as moorland slopes take over. Though it is easy to rise directly to the cairned minor top of Pen y Manllwyn, ahead, a far more rewarding route keeps left at a fork before the direct path up the flank merges in. The splendid path curves around the head of Cwm y Nant before moving away towards the end. When a small cairn appears above, the path can be abandoned to climb the few feet to a higher level one just behind the cairn.

Doubling back right a similarly benign pull leads south-east over Pen y Manllwyn, with the big summit dome of Waun Fach just ahead. The well worn path curves around the head of a cwm to the beckoning upper slopes, which briefly steepen to gain the vast summit plateau. Rather handily the highest point is just yards ahead, where the remains of a trig. point base flounder in an otherwise featureless scene. Views are notable only in their extent, for there is nothing of interest in the immediate vicinity, save for the shapely top of Pen y Gadair Fawr to the south-east. This tempts a worthwhile walk out, requiring an hour or so for the return trip. The down-side is a crossing of the pathless and moist plateau before a clear path forms. This descends to a broad, peaty col which is soon negotiated to gain the firmer slopes of the short climb. The summit dome appears unnatural, and certainly the cairn is given antiquity status.

Storm clouds over Waun Fach, from near Pengenfford

Pen y Gadair Fawr is inferior to Waun Fach in height only, for its summit rewards the walker with a well earned contrast to that of its parent fell. A sizeable cairn marks this grand spot, and firm grass offers a welcome seat to survey the panorama. Best features of the long Black Mountains' ridges are the shapely Pen Cerrig-calch and Pen Allt-mawr to the south-west, while even Waun Fach itself appears something like a mountain. The high Brecon Beacons rise to the west, and perhaps the one disappointment is the proximity of a plantation south of this viewpoint, remarkable for this altitude.

Waun Fach's summit is departed south-west, a clear path forming within a hundred yards. This steady descent levels out to curve round onto Pen Trumau, an improving stride which offers a super prospect of Waun Fach and Pen y Gadair Fawr. The path descends pleasantly to a meeting place of paths on a well defined bwlch. An historic old way crossing the ridge at this point tenders itself as a first-class descent route from the hills.

The western arm of this bridleway doubles back sharply north-west, and keeping left on the main path at an early fork, soon slants down the slopes of Rhiw Trumau above the scattered farms and fields of The Forest. With Castell Dinas increasingly dominant ahead, the path curves down to the base of the open slopes. Now enclosed, it descends between pastures, the lower section a super old holloway between hollies before emerging onto a back road.

To the right the road quickly forks, and the left branch drops down to a trekking centre at Cwmfforest before climbing back out. Descending again at a hairpin bend, a rough old way advances straight on: this is the byway on which the walk began, rising pleasantly to pass a couple of houses before returning to the rear of the pub.

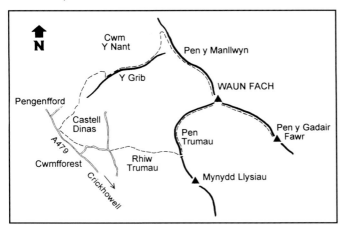

PEN Y FAN 2907ft/886m
WAUN RYDD 2523ft/769m

Pen y Fan is the highest peak in Britain south of Cadair Idris, a fitting apex to the relatively unsung Brecon Beacons. While the Beacons are just one hill group in this mountainous National Park, the high tops clustered around Pen y Fan are without doubt the most popular. Gentle slopes rise from the south, and the modest escarpments that line the southern edges of these plateaux give no indication of the grandeur of their abrupt northerly termini, where weathered sandstone tiers plunge to the pastures of the Usk valley.

The pinnacle of South Wales' mountains is shadowed by its partner Corn Du, a minor top yet without whose kinship Pen y Fan would be less of a mountain. More in keeping with the main peak, its easterly underling of Cribyn provides a summit again looking sharp from the north, retaining a typical Beacons profile. Looking eastwards this aspect is repeated a third time on a still lower peak, the more modest Fan y Big. These hills all send appealing ridges falling northwards, bounding wild cwms that relent to wooded feeders of the Usk. Interestingly it is the minor top, Corn Du, that sends the most diverse ridge north, curving down to Pen Milan and enclosing the only sheet of water, Llyn Cwm Llwch.

The mountains are split by an ancient road running north between Cribyn and Fan y Big, the most direct route from Merthyr to Brecon. Unfortunately it retains some of this original status, and at certain times vehicles are permitted along its rough surface. So don't be surprised if in March, September or October you encounter a 4x4 hero negotiating his charge through the Bwlch ar y Fan at almost 2000ft. This irrepressible escarpment resumes eastwards yet again towards the final peak, the unassuming Waun Rydd.

Unfortunately this hill cannot maintain the impressive profile of its colleagues, though it does still offer an engaging northern ridge, and fine views from less exciting plateau edges to east and south.

Of many ascent routes, northern approaches are the most traditional, western ones the easiest, and southern ones the most intriguing. All northern ridges can be approached by leafy lanes from Brecon, culminating in sequestered farms at the base of these spurs. Pen y Fan's own Cefn Cwm Llwch is the finest, steepening to a minor clamber to emerge impeccably onto the very summit.

Pen Milan, adjacent ridge to the west, gives another route, though the start is usually varied by heading first into Cwm Llwch to take in its little lake before slanting up to the Tommy Jones Obelisk on the ridge. This landmark recalls the touching story of a five year old boy who became lost looking for his father in 1900, and perished from exhaustion. Above the obelisk the path treads the rim up onto Corn Du, which is also the first objective of the following routes from the west.

A worn path climbs from the Storey Arms outdoor centre on the A470, dropping to cross the Blaen Taf Fawr before a moorland rise to gain Craig Cwm Llwch above the obelisk. The blocky corner of Corn Du's plateau presents a simple obstacle to gaining its flat top, with Pen y Fan just a short stride away. Another path leaves a car park a little further south to slant across to Bwlch Duwynt, a classic moment as Pen y Fan is revealed with the Black Mountains far beyond. Corn Du can be omitted, or scaled by the diminutive blocks of its brief south ridge. A variant path also leaves the rim above the obelisk to gain the Bwlch Duwynt. These western approaches offer elevated starts at more than 1300ft/400m.

Routes from the south spring from the Taf Fechan and Tal-y-Bont Forests. From the former, the old road through the Bwlch ar y Fan is an easy stride above the Neuadd reservoirs to gain the ridge, where a path traverses Cribyn's southern flank to set its short sights on Pen y Fan. From the dam of the lower reservoir a path ascends moorland slopes to a steep pull onto the Graig Fan Ddu ridge to the west, and enjoys a well earned easy stride north to Corn Du and Pen y Fan. From the Tal-y-Bont Forest a high level start sees a quick way onto Craig y Fan Ddu, the southern spur of a broad plateau attached to Waun Rydd. It offers an easy route onto that summit with the bonus of being well placed to savour an extended march around the northern scarps to Pen y Fan itself.

Waun Rydd is the unfrequented hill of the group, but can be enjoyed individually on several ascent lines. A route from Aber to the east scales the broad ridge of Twyn Du to the landmark of Carn Pica on the edge of the summit plateau; a little further south, by Talybont Reservoir, a bridleway gives access to slopes rising to the minor top of Allt Lwyd, from where a short ridge gives a gentle rise onto the plateau. To the north, lanes leaving the villages of Llanfrynach and Pencelli send enclosed paths between pastures onto the sprawling slopes of Bryn, above which an improving ridge leads above Cwm Cwareli on the Rhiw Bwlch y Ddwyallt.

ROUTE 30: PEN Y FAN & WAUN RYDD

Summits:
Waun Rydd   2523ft/769m
Fan y Big   2359ft/719m
Cribyn   2608ft/795m
Pen y Fan   2907ft/886m

Start: *Tal-y-Bont Forest (SO 056175). Forest Enterprise Torpantau car park on the summit of a minor road linking Pontsticill, north of Merthyr Tydfil, with Talybont-on-Usk. Pontsticill is served by bus from Merthyr Tydfil, Talybont-on-Usk is served by Brecon-Abergavenny buses.*

Distance: *12½ miles/20km*   **Ascent:** *3070ft/936m*

Maps:
OS 1:50,000 - Landranger 160. 1:25,000 - Outdoor Leisure 12

Where the rough road crosses a stream to enter the car park, a path climbs north above the ravine. A trio of beautiful waterfalls see the walk off to a mercurial start, and after the fence turns away the ravine also relents, a moorland stream meandering the upper reaches. The path climbs to a distinct halt on the brow of Craig y Fan Ddu, already marking the end of any appreciable work for a considerable time. With suitable timing, Corn Du and Pen y Fan assert their upper contours over to the left.

A cairn marks a fork in the path on the southern tip of this plateau, and the well worn right branch crosses to the eastern rim to enjoy a wide sweep over the side valley to the tame slopes of Waun Rydd. A simple progression north along the edge of the modest yet steep scarp begins, a prelude to the more impressive scarps that will follow.

While Talybont Reservoir is seen down to the right, distant Pen y Fan plays hide and seek during this section, as the peaty first half gives way to improving conditions. The path runs on to the inevitable moment where it reaches a path junction at Bwlch y Ddwyallt. Immediately there are extensive views north over Cwm Cwareli to a seemingly endless spread of mid Wales.

To the west the Beacons escarpment and ridges supply all the temptations, but a short detour onto Waun Rydd awaits. The path doubling back up the easy if slightly peaty slopes on the right soon eases out on the top, and doubling back north, the broad top is crossed to the waiting cairn. This last stage enjoys a complete panorama of the Black Mountains beyond Llangorse Lake.

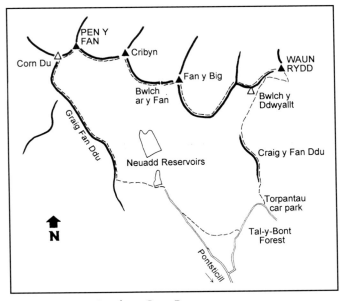

Opposite: Pen y Fan from Corn Du

Craig y Fan Ddu on the southern approach to Waun Rydd

A bee-line from the cairn back to the bwlch joins an unmissable path contouring west and clinging faithfully to the rim above Cwm Cwareli. A faint rise leads past the cairn on Bwlch y Ddwyallt, quite outstanding walking with the high Beacons beckoning. A big sweep works round above Cwm Oergwm to descend to a col before Fan y Big, with both Neuadd reservoirs in view down to the left. Here at Craig Cwmoergwm, piles of quarried stone have been fashioned into shelters.

While a path bears off to omit Fan y Big, far better to enjoy the grassy rise high above Cwm Oergwm for an easy stroll to the summit. Here a rock platform claims an airy stance looking over Cwm Cynwyn to the next objective, Cribyn, while the ridge of Cefn Cyff runs down to the north. A good path works back down the western edge, a short drop to Bwlch ar y Fan through which runs the rough track of the old Merthyr-Brecon road. A steep haul up the opposite slope is redeemed by the prospect of an easy rise around the rim of Craig Cwm Cynwyn to Cribyn's summit, though the return to the scene of Pen y Fan is an even greater spur. Cribyn offers another neat top, with its northern ridge, Bryn Teg, falling away initially steeply and roughly.

There is no denying Pen y Fan any longer, and a well pitched path descends south-west, savouring the terraced sandstone face of the principal peak. Resuming ascent mode at once, the part pitched path is joined by the short-cut, and a steep climb leads through a few blocky outcrops onto Pen y Fan's summit plateau. Invariably the northern rim is followed to its apex to look down on another typical northern ridge before turning the few yards inland to the large cairn. At this point the Carmarthen Fan finally appear, very distant beyond the westernmost summits of Fforest Fawr. A clear day sees Exmoor rising across the Severn Estuary, but perhaps the highlight is the simple but brilliant mix of valleys and rolling hills leading northwards.

On the western rim the well worn path bound for Corn Du (2864ft/873m) is picked up. The inevitable by-pass cuts round to its left, but this minor top deserves the few feet of well blazed ascent to renew acquaintance with a northern scarp, and a good vantage point for the parent fell. Beyond its cairn a path turns south along an abrupt little edge, at the end descending through more minor outcrops to the path junction at Bwlch Duwynt.

Continuing south, a path rises onto the Craig Gwaun Taf ridge, and the walk's final escarpment is a surprisingly fine one despite the lack of any appreciable summits. A clear path runs high above the valley head, with the Neuadd reservoirs glistening below. The narrow ridge of Rhiw yr Ysgyfarnog develops, with views down into valleys on both sides. A cairn is passed just to the right and the way runs on above Graig Fan Ddu. The point to leave comes just after a big curve back in to the right, where a massive cairn stands over a tiny but distinctive stream crossing. An OS column at point 642m can be seen further down the ridge.

An initially rough path descends with the stream, soon easing on grassier slopes to drop onto a marshy shelf. Beyond this the path improves to slant down to a gate off the hill, leading to a colourful crossing of the grassy embankment of Lower Neuadd Reservoir. A footbridge at the end sends a path up onto an access road, and through a gate on the right this rises to a crossroads of ways: that coming in from the left is the rough road through the Bwlch ar y Fan.

As the surfaced road drops away, a more inviting bridle track contours along to the left. This is the course of a railway built to aid construction of the Neuadd reservoirs, and runs a delightful course beneath the plantations to join a forest road. This advances on to reach the through road at the site of Torpantau station, at a junction with the former Merthyr-Talybont-Brecon Railway: this tunnelled under the pass just beneath the road here. A short climb leads to the road summit, with the car park just in front.

FAN BRYCHEINIOG   2631ft/802m

The westernmost mountain peaks of southern Wales are collectively known as the Carmarthen Fan, and they exhibit the same general features as the true Brecon Beacons centred on Pen y Fan, further to the east. The Black Mountain (Mynydd Du) is the regular title for this vast upland sweep, though walkers are only normally found embracing the remarkable escarpments falling north to sweeps of moorland and encroaching forestry.

Heading for the Afon Twrch; Fan Brycheiniog and Fan Hir behind

While these incredible scarps plunge with the same Old Red Sandstone character of the Beacons, their gently declining southern slopes soon arrive at a great plateau of Carboniferous Limestone, an area that sees as many cavers as hillwalkers. The welcome presence of limestone is experienced by most visitors at the roadside Dan yr Ogof showcaves, but walkers striding out along the old bridleway from Glyntawe can experience these gleaming white rocks for free. Beneath these inviting uplands is a cave system surpassed only by the Three Counties System under Leck Fell on the western edge of the Yorkshire Dales.

The heart of the Carmarthen Fan lies firmly along the aforementioned sandstone scarp, which runs a rather erratic course supporting various mountain summits. At the core of this is the major dog-leg centred on Fan Brycheiniog ('Breconshire upland'). This is the principal peak, its main support being Picws Du, otherwise known as Bannau Sir Gaer ('Carmarthenshire upland'): the traditional county boundary runs between the two. The unsung yet remarkable Fan Hir completes the triumvirate, though away from the escarpments there are other summits to the west, with Garreg Las offering excellent walking.

This exceptional scarp is further enhanced by the presence of two mountain lakes, often seen only as dark pools in shadowy hollows, but infusing stronger character into this already atmospheric place. A legend attached to the smaller Llyn y Fan Fach tells the tragic love story of a 'Lady in the Lake', her marriage to a local lad ending in despair when she returned beneath the waters. Additionally, the extensive slopes of Fan Brycheiniog give rise to two of southern Wales' great rivers, the Tawe and the Usk.

Fan Brycheiniog offers two summits of equal height, one boasting a trig. point and shelter, the other, known as Twr y Fan Foel, with just a scrappy cairn to mark its superior stance on a tiny spur. Across the Bwlch Blaen-Twrch to the west, the highest point on Picws Du sends the weathered Bannau Sir Gaer scarp on a very gentle yet dramatic course to a minor top, before the ridge curves round to mark the end of the escarpment.

The shortest approach to Fan Brycheiniog is from the crest of the Glyntawe-Trecastle road to the east. A path leaves Bwlch Cerrig Duon at 1562ft/476m, and runs south-west to rise gently to the southern shore of Llyn y Fan Fawr, thence climbing to the ridge-path at Bwlch y Giedd between Fan Brycheiniog and Fan Hir. From Llanddeusant to the north, a route uses the cul-de-sac lane up the course of the Afon Sawdde, becoming the access road to the filter house at the dam of Llyn y Fan Fach. Confronted by the dark walls of the scarps, a path slants up to gain the western rim of Bannau Sir Gaer, thence curving round towards Picws Du.

The direct route from the south also takes in an earlier summit, Fan Hir, en route to the major peak. Crossing the Tawe by a footbridge from the Tafarn-y-Garreg pub on the A4067, a permitted path gains the open hill just north of Ty Hendrey, and climbs steeply before settling down to a steady and remarkable rise atop the Fan Hir escarpment. The modest Bwlch y Giedd links it to Fan Brycheiniog. The best initial approach starts just a little further south at Glyntawe, where a bridleway crosses the ravine

of the Afon Haffes to begin a fascinating march through limestone country. As the old path fades there are numerous ways of gaining the unseen escarpment across the tame southern slopes. In order to savour the scarp to the full it is best to work round to its western limit, but a more direct route leads up to the Cwar-du-bach bwlch, where a cairn signifies a sudden, dramatic moment as the profile of Bannau Sir Gaer is revealed, with Llyn y Fan Fach below.

ROUTE 31: FAN BRYCHEINIOG

Summits:
Bannau Sir Gaer   2457ft/749m
Fan Brycheiniog   2631ft/802m
Fan Hir   2497ft/761m

Start: Glyntawe (SN 846165). Lay-bys on the A4067 Sennybridge to Swansea road by the Tafarn-y-Garreg pub; roadside parking on the old road alongside the Gwyn Arms pub. Served by Brecon-Swansea buses.

Distance: 11½ miles/18½km   **Ascent:** 2822ft/860m

Maps:
OS 1:50,000 - Landranger 160. 1:25,000 - Outdoor Leisure 12

A bridleway leaves the road a little south of Tawe Bridge, as an access road to Carreg Haffes. Beyond the house a track rises past trees to gain the bank of the Afon Haffes in a wide stony gorge. When in spate, the bridleway can be gained from a path starting by the Dan-yr-Ogof showcaves. Safely across, the bridleway slants up the bracken hillside away from the ravine, enjoying early views over the upper Tawe valley with shapely Cribarth to the south.

After the accompanying wall is replaced by a fence, a grassy branch forks right at a brow, before the track reaches its high point. Another right branch at an early fork points towards a craggy knoll on the skyline, but swinging right, the way merges into a broader grassy track to resume north-west. This super way runs on through some splendid limestone scenery. The southern slopes of Fan Hir are soon seen rising beyond the limestone over to the right.

Passing some shakeholes the way rises gently before a more level walk above the boggy basin of Waun Fignen Felen, backed by the currently featureless Carmarthen Fan. At a fork the more level right arm runs through a minor bwlch and past attractive pools around Pwll y Cig to reach an appreciable stream. A thinner path climbs the slope beyond, fading as it crosses the brow of Twyn Tal y Ddraenen. Ahead is the broad upper valley of the Afon Twrch, while southwards are the countless knolls and hollows of an unfrequented rolling landscape. Sheep and pony trods now lead down to a crook in the more noteworthy Afon Twrch. Across, a grassy path runs downstream to another bend, where an inflowing stream is crossed beneath an old sheepfold. An initially faint way rises across the southern flank of Bannau Sir Gaer, to gradually contour more clearly north-west to the bwlch at Pen-Rhiw-goch.

With rugged Carreg yr Ogof (1919ft/585m) in front, the empty slopes of Bannau Sir Gaer's west top, Waun Lefrith, can be scaled. A more rewarding option slants further north to gain the ridge at the rim enclosing Llyn y Fan Fach, a champagne moment as the higher peaks are ranged beyond this lake. Either way, a cairn at 2221ft/677m will be found to share this minor top with its own sizeable pool. Now transformed, the route forges eastwards along the crest of the escarpment, dropping imperceptibly before a more prolonged rise onto Picws Du, summit of Bannau Sir Gaer.

The summit cairn stands just a stride from the edge on an ancient mound, and reveals the impending slopes of the major hill of the group, with both its 802m cairns evident. A descent east to Bwlch Blaen-Twrch precedes a longer rise, slanting above an intriguingly inclined scarp onto easier ground. The path runs on to a cairn on another minor top, Fan Foel. Looking back, Bannau Sir Gaer makes a fine study with Llyn y Fan Fach beyond.

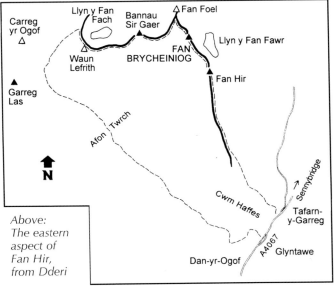

Above: The eastern aspect of Fan Hir, from Dderi

High on the Carmarthen Fan: Bannau Sir Gaer from Waun Lefrith

Also revealed is the splendid prospect of the upper scarp of Twr y Fan Foel, Fan Brycheiniog's northern twin summit. Skirting past a pool to the south-east, a tiny rise onto this airy stance earns another superb moment. The two highest tops of the Brecon Beacons rise imperiously to the east beyond Fforest Fawr, while at the very foot of the escarpment are the waters of Llyn y Fan Fawr.

Two minutes south along the edge are the OS column and a circular shelter. The return simply resumes along the edge, with a descent to Bwlch y Giedd preceding a short pull onto Fan Hir. This proves a real bonus of a scarp walk, running south-east past tiny outcrops to a minute summit cairn. On again, the path runs gently south atop a very uniform scarp, largely grassy yet virtually sheer. Passing through some scattered boulders the edge falters, but the path maintains the same line over slightly steeper slopes, then onto easier ground to pass the knoll of Allt Fach.

With the finish revealed below, the path slants more steeply down towards Ty Hendrey. As a sunken way it delves into bracken, with a steeper direct branch down to the farm. A permitted path goes left of concrete pens, just beneath which an enclosed trackway runs down to the river Tawe. A short stroll downstream past a sizeable confluence leads to a footbridge, across which the path runs on to join the main road opposite the Tafarn-y-Garreg pub.

124

FOEL-FRAS 3091ft/942m

To the north of Carnedd Llewelyn, the vast rolling crest of the Carneddau spills over many an untramped mile towards the Aber Falls and the Bwlch y Ddeufaen. Though less exciting than the heights above Ogwen, they offer no less than three 3000ft summits, numerous other substantial tops, and a character very much their own. These hills are typified by steep slopes rising to high plateaux, with most of the summits being extensive but given a dash of colour by a variety of rock formations, from mere rashes of stones to more impressive clusters of outcrops, as on Bera Mawr.

Though all three high tops are subservient to Carnedd Llewelyn, the northernmost, Foel-fras, stakes an optimistic claim to 'Munro' status, on a par with some rounded tops of the eastern Grampians. It is best known as a scene of great celebrations, for its trig. point marks the northerly terminus of the Welsh 3000-footers walk, a marathon challenge commencing on the top of Snowdon and incorporating the other 13 summits in between.

Foel Grach is but a minor blip under the northern slopes of Carnedd Llewelyn, and is probably best known for its refuge, an emergency hut occupying arguably the most remote summit in the Carneddau, if not the entire Welsh mountains. It is to be found huddled beneath a tumble of boulders defending the summit to the north. Least significant summit is the central one, Garnedd Uchaf, being overtopped by both its colleagues and rising barely a hundred feet above the great ridge.

Ascent routes spring from east, west and north, the latter being most popular with its inducement of a visit to the accessible Aber Falls. These make a pleasant short objective to the south of the coastal village of Abergwyngregyn (Aber). For the devotee of wide open spaces they are merely a springboard to the tops: a wealth of minor trods lead up grassy slopes towards the summits of Drosgl, Bera Mawr and Llwytmor. The latter is linked directly to Foel-fras, while Drosgl and Bera Mawr are spawned by Garnedd Uchaf. To the north-east of these tops a long curving ridge climbs from above Aber onto Drum, another link to Foel-fras.

Easterly approaches stem from a minor road above the Conwy Valley, serving the entrance to Cwm Eigiau. An eastern shoulder that belongs as much to Carnedd Llewelyn as to Foel Grach offers a fine way up above the cwm holding Melynllyn. Above Roewen the Bwlch y Ddeufaen gives a leg-up onto Drum, while to its south a way traverses the flank of Pen y Castell en route to the upper slopes of Foel-fras. The hills can also be easily approached from the west by way of Bethesda either onto Gyrn Wigau, a shoulder of Drosgl, or into the valley of the Afon Caseg.

Walkers leaving Foel Grach for Garnedd Uchaf

ROUTE 32: FOEL-FRAS

Summits:
Bera Mawr   2605ft/794m
Garnedd Uchaf   3038ft/926m
Foel Grach   3202ft/976m
Foel-fras   3091ft/942m
Drum   2526ft/770m

Start: *Abergwyngregyn (SH 663719). Forestry Commission car park above Bont Newydd, south of Abergwyngregyn village off the A55. The village is served by Caernarfon-Bangor-Conwy-Llandudno buses, with a rail station at Llanfairfechan 2 miles to the east.*

Distance: *12 miles/19km*   **Ascent:** *3500ft/1067m*

Maps:
OS 1:50,000 - Landranger 115. 1:25,000 - Outdoor Leisure 17

From Bont Newydd a path runs upstream to a footbridge, crossing the Afon Rhaeadr-fawr to resume upstream on a broad access track. A similar track descends from the main car park, and merged they run on to reveal a first view of the upper section of Aber Falls beneath the serrated crest of Bera Mawr. The restored farmhouse at Nant Rhaeadr is soon reached, now a small visitor centre within the Coedydd Aber National Nature Reserve. The track rises through open country between woodland and runs on through glorious surrounds to the base of the falls, a beautiful scene.

From a stile on the left, a good path slants back up beneath scree slopes, meeting a junction at the edge of the plantation. Doubling back right a path contours through the scree, with good views of the falls and of Moel Wnion (1903ft/580m) rising across the valley. Beyond the scree the path enjoys a lively crossing of a ravine and runs on through a potentially dangerous section where water floods across the path. The drama is left behind as the upper

valley of the Afon Goch is entered. Negotiating the stream with caution, a number of sheep/pony trods work up the steep slope opposite to gain the foot of this broad northerly ridge of Bera Mawr.

Easy strides up the untracked rough grass pass the stone circular bases of ancient settlements, and the notched skyline soon returns to draw steps up through boulders to the summit of Bera Mawr. This fascinating top is the finest in the Carneddau, and the highest point demands a minor scramble on its east side. The view north looks over the northern end of the Menai Strait to Anglesey and Priestholm, with Northern Ireland's Mountains of Mourne visible on a clear day. Neighbouring hills include the slightly higher but less impressive twin Bera Bach.

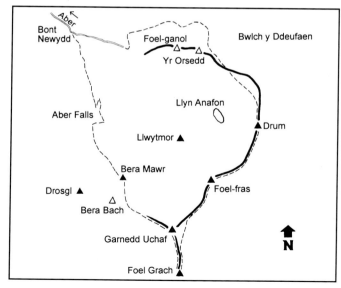

Back down through the rocks, gently rising slopes around the rear of Bera Bach lead to a clear path ascending to the waiting tor of Yr Aryg. From here it is just a short pull onto Garnedd Uchaf, first of the 3000-footers. A rocky crest salvages the inadequacy of the plateau top, with Foel Grach waiting to the south in front of Carnedd Llewelyn. However, it is the fine peak of Yr Elen and its ridges to the right of Carnedd Llewelyn that catch the eye.

To the east of the rocks a well worn path descends to the minor bwlch from where it is a short climb to the Foel Grach refuge, and the tumble of rocks behind it lead onto another broad summit plateau. A massive pile of stones sits at the northern edge, though the finest aspect is again south, to Yr Elen with the neat peak of Elidir Fawr behind. The all-round view provides a splendid contrast, in the coastline of both the mainland and Anglesey. Garnedd Uchaf's lack of status is underlined in its insignificance from here, being overtopped by Foel-fras.

Back at the bwlch with Garnedd Uchaf, a three-way split offers the right branch as a bee-line for Foel-fras. Contouring around Garnedd Uchaf's eastern flank, it falters a little before meeting the ridge path on a shelf. A moist area is crossed before the gentle rise onto Foel-fras, an unanticipated wall leading north to the summit. A useful stone shelter is passed en route to the Ordnance Survey column amid rashes of stones. A distant cry from the mountain wall to the south is the prospect of the coastal resort of Llandudno beneath the Great Orme headland.

Resuming, the wall ends as suddenly as it arrived, and a fence leads the path down big slopes to a bwlch before a very gentle pull past a couple of minor outcrops onto Drum. The massive summit pile of stones (a circular shelter) stands across the fence, while looking back, Foel-fras blocks out the rest of high mountain country. Continuing north, a track is found to run just west of the fence, offering a foolproof descent route. Passing through a bwlch onto the east side of the ridge, two other options await.

The slopes on the left descend to the Llyn Anafon access road, while surplus energy can be spent by clinging to high ground over the descending ridge featuring the shapely tops of Yr Orsedd and Foel-ganol.

The track, meanwhile, offers a fine leg-stretching tramp down above the unfrequented slopes of the side valley, ultimately meeting the Roman road coming through the Bwlch y Ddeufaen at a crossroads in front of pylons. This identical track leads west, dropping down to eventually become surfaced. This narrow lane continues down to the valley floor to return to Bont Newydd.

Foel-fras from Bera Mawr